0780

(War)
821
(War)

STUDIES ~~IN ECONOMIC AND SOCIAL HISTO~~RY

This series, specially commissioned by the Economic History Society, provides a guide to the current interpretations of the key themes of economic and social history in which advances have recently been made or in which there has been significant debate.

Originally entitled 'Studies in Economic History', in 1974 the series had its scope extended to include topics in social history, and the new series title, 'Studies in Economic and Social History', signalises this development.

The series gives readers access to the best work done, helps them to draw their own conclusions in major fields of study, and by means of the critical bibliography in each book guides them in the selection of further reading. The aim is to provide a springboard to further work rather than a set of pre-packaged conclusions or short-cuts.

This ECONOMIC HISTORY SOCIETY

The Economic History Society, which numbers ~~over 3000~~ ~~members, pub~~lishes the *Economic History Review* four times a year (free to members) and holds an annual conference. Enquiries about membership should be addressed to the Assistant Secretary, Economic History Society, Peterhouse, Cambridge. Full-time students may join at special rates.

STUDIES IN ECONOMIC AND SOCIAL HISTORY

Edited for the Economic History Society by L. A. Clarkson

PUBLISHED

Bill Albert Latin America and the World Economy from Independence to 1930
B. W. E. Alford Depression and Recovery? British Economic Growth, 1918–1939
Michael Anderson Approaches to the History of the Western Family, 1500–1914
P. J. Cain Economic Foundations of British Overseas Expansion, 1815–1914
S. D. Chapman The Cotton Industry in the Industrial Revolution
Neil Charlesworth British Rule and the Indian Economy, 1800–1914
J. A. Chartres Internal Trade in England, 1500–1700
R. A. Church The Great Victorian Boom, 1850–1873
L. A. Clarkson Proto-Industrialization: The First Phase of Industrialization?
D. C. Coleman Industry in Tudor and Stuart England
P. L. Cottrell British Overseas Investment in the Nineteenth Century
Ralph Davis English Overseas Trade, 1500–1700
M. E. Falkus The Industrialisation of Russia, 1700–1914
Peter Fearon The Origins and Nature of the Great Slump, 1929–1932
T. R. Gourvish Railways and the British Economy, 1830–1914
Robert Gray The Aristocracy of Labour in Nineteenth-century Britain, c.1850–1900
John Hatcher Plague, Population and the English Economy, 1348–1530
J. R. Hay The Origins of the Liberal Welfare Reforms, 1906–1914
R. H. Hilton The Decline of Serfdom in Medieval England
E. L. Jones The Development of English Agriculture, 1815–1873
John Lovell British Trade Unions, 1875–1933
Hugh McLeod Religion and the Working Class in Nineteenth-Century Britain
J. D. Marshall The Old Poor Law, 1795–1834
Alan S. Milward The Economic Effects of the Two World Wars on Britain
G. E. Mingay Enclosure and the Small Farmer in the Age of the Industrial Revolution
Rosalind Mitchison British Population Change Since 1860
R. J. Morris Class and Class Consciousness in the Industrial Revolution, 1780–1850
J. Forbes Munro Britain in Tropical Africa, 1880–1960
A. E. Musson British Trade Unions, 1880–1975
R. B. Outhwaite Inflation in Tudor and Early Stuart England
R. J. Overy The Nazi Economic Recovery, 1932–1938
P. L. Payne British Entrepreneurship in the Nineteenth Century
G. D. Ramsay The English Woollen Industry, 1500–1750
Michael E. Rose The Relief of Poverty, 1834–1914
Michael Sanderson Education, Economic Change and Society in England 1780–1870
S. B. Saul The Myth of the Great Depression, 1873–1896
Arthur J. Taylor Laissez-faire and State Intervention in Nineteenth-century Britain
Peter Temin Causal Factors in American Economic Growth in the Nineteenth Century
Michael Turner Enclosures in Britain, 1750–1830
Margaret Walsh The American Frontier Revisited
J. R. Ward Poverty and Progress in the Caribbean, 1800–1960

OTHER TITLES ARE IN PREPARATION

Poverty and Progress in the Caribbean 1800–1960

Prepared for
The Economic History Society by

J.R. WARD

Lecturer in Economic History
University of Edinburgh

MACMILLAN

First published 1985

Published by
Higher and Further Education Division
MACMILLAN PUBLISHERS LTD
Houndmills, Basingstoke, Hampshire RG21 2XS
and London
Companies and representatives
throughout the world

Printed in Hong Kong

British Library Cataloguing in Publication Data
Ward, J. R.
Poverty and progress in the Caribbean 1800–1960.
—(Studies in economic and social history)
1. Caribbean Area—Economic conditions
I. Title   II. Series
330.9182'1   HC151
ISBN 0–333–37212–3

Contents

List of Tables, Map and Graph

Note on References

References in the text within square brackets relate to the numbered items in the Select Bibliography, followed, where necessary, by the page number in italics, for example (1:*45*]. The other references, numbered consecutively, relate to the items specified in the Notes section.

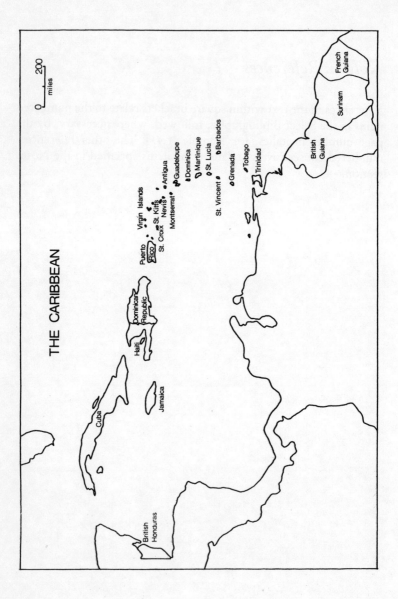

THE CARIBBEAN

British Honduras

Cuba

Jamaica

Haiti

Dominican Republic

Puerto Rico

Virgin Islands

St. Croix

St. Kitts

Nevis

Montserrat

Antigua

Guadeloupe

Dominica

Martinique

St. Lucia

St. Vincent

Barbados

Grenada

Tobago

Trinidad

British Guiana

Surinam

French Guiana

0   200
     miles

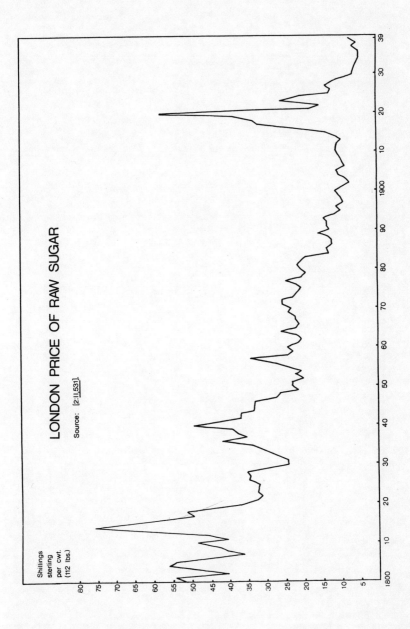

LONDON PRICE OF RAW SUGAR

Source: [2:11,531].

Shillings
sterling
per cwt.
(112 lbs.)

9

Editor's Preface

When this series was established in 1968 the first editor, the late Professor M. W. Flinn, laid down three guiding principles. The books should be concerned with important fields of economic history; they should be surveys of the current state of scholarship rather than a vehicle for the specialist views of the authors; and, above all, they were to be introductions to their subject and not 'a set of pre-packaged conclusions'. These aims were admirably fulfilled by Professor Flinn and by his successor, Professor T. C. Smout, who took over the series in 1977. As it passes to its third editor and approaches its third decade, the principles remain the same.

Nevertheless, times change, even though principles do not. The series was launched when the study of economic history was burgeoning and new findings and fresh interpretations were threatening to overwhelm students – and sometimes their teachers. The series has expanded its scope, particularly in the area of social history – although the distinction between 'economic' and 'social' is sometimes hard to recognise and even more difficult to sustain. It has also extended geographically; its roots remain firmly British, but an increasing number of titles is concerned with the economic and social history of the wider world. However, some of the early titles can no longer claim to be introductions to the current state of scholarship; and the discipline as a whole lacks the heady growth of the 1960s and early 1970s. To overcome the first problem a number of new editions, or entirely new works, have been commissioned – some have already appeared. To deal with the second, the aim remains to publish up-to-date introductions to important areas of debate. If the series can demonstrate to students and their teachers the importance of the discipline of economic and social history and excite its further study, it will continue the task so ably begun by its first two editors.

L.A. CLARKSON
The Queen's University of Belfast   Editor

11

1 Introduction

The modern Caribbean is sometimes described as 'underdeveloped' or 'developing', part of the 'Third World', and calculations of production per head of population (see Table I) suggest that such terms are reasonable.[1] Clearly, however, there are wide variations in fortune within the region. A few territories seem quite prosperous by international standards, and only Haiti approaches the acute poverty of tropical Africa or South Asia. Nevertheless it is still useful to consider the Caribbean as a whole, to emphasise its recurrent and distinctive features.

First, it has a shared experience of discovery and occupation by European colonists from the end of the fifteenth century. These newcomers exterminated the native inhabitants and imported large numbers of African slaves, whose descendants became a principal element of population. This is in contrast to most other areas of European colonisation, where either a substantial native population remained (as in Africa, Asia and much of continental Latin America), or non-Europeans were only a minority among the immigrants (as in North America, Australia and Argentina). Second, most of the Caribbean has at one time or another been heavily committed to an export crop, usually sugar, which lends itself particularly to large-scale plantation production. Third, it is composed of islands[2], none of more than medium size, a geographical fact that has reinforced their tendency to specialise in a single export staple and has prolonged their colonial status. So while European nations have held other colonies, many of them heavily reliant upon coerced labour and considerable exporters of tropical produce, nowhere else have slavery, plantations and colonial rule together had such sustained or pervasive influence.

This survey will consider problems raised by some of the main contributions to the economic history of the Caribbean, from the last generations of slavery to the Cuban Revolution of 1959 and the granting of political independence to the main British colonies in the early 1960s. Attention will be focused upon the evolution of

13

Table I

Levels of Gross Domestic Product per Head of Population (in 1976 US dollars)

	1950	1960	1970	1976
Puerto Rico	946	1 497	2 689	2 804
Trinidad and Tobago	—	1 165	1 228	2 320
Surinam	—	839	1 145	1 710
Barbados	472	671	1 017	1 605
Jamaica	395	839	1 095	1 443
Cuba	917	964[a]	—	899
Dominican Republic	472	459	534	814
Antigua	—	—	—	563
Guyana	531	585	548	556
Grenada	—	—	—	396
Haiti	—	145	136	218
Kenya	166	192	208	243
Indonesia	133	160	—	285
Mexico	470	641	972	1 096
United Kingdom	2 382	2 631	3 217	3 951
United States	4 657	5 434	6 992	7 879

[a] Estimate for 1958.

Sources: World Bank, *World Tables* (2nd edn, Baltimore, 1980); The Economist, *The World in Figures* (2nd edn, 1978); [88: *74*; 89: *509, 1046*].

sugar production and some of its wider consequences within the region. Sugar planting based upon slavery had come to dominate most territories by the later eighteenth or early nineteenth centuries, but then the slaves were freed, at different times, in different ways, and with many different results. In some cases after emancipation the plantations remained and even flourished, while in others they failed and were replaced by small-scale peasant farmers. Often, however, a middle course was followed between these two extremes, with a proportion of the plantations surviving alongside a peasantry. Chapters 2 and 3 examine these topics. The subject of Chapter 4 is economic development, defined as the growth of income or production per head and diversification away from agriculture. While some development has been achieved within the Caribbean it has in general been very limited by the standards of Europe or North America. The consequences of this were felt with particular severity in the difficult international economic conditions of the 1920s and 1930s, and extensive popular disturbances resulted. In response, colonial authorities and local politicians introduced various reforming measures which, combined with other favourable influences, achieved considerable successes in some islands during the 1940s and 1950s, but very little in others. More recently over much of the region the rate of economic development has tended to slow down. What are the causes of this modern pattern of both real progresss and persistent poverty? How much emphasis should be given, for example, to the legacy of slavery, or to geographical fragmentation and limited natural resources as handicaps? Is it true, as some argue, that successful capitalist development is impossible for economies which have been dominated by plantations? What were the implications of colonial status?

For a long time historical writing on the Caribbean lacked both quality and quantity. Most was the work of Europeans or North Americans, not especially knowledgeable or sympathetic, and strongly influenced by their own preoccupations with, for example, the ethics of slavery [3; 8]. Moreover, during the nineteenth century the region lost in the eyes of outsiders the importance it once had as the world's principal source of tropical exports and as a focus of international rivalries. More recently much has been done to remedy this neglect. Centres of scholarship have developed within the Caribbean, and these are naturally more willing to take the region as a subject of interest in its own right. They have been reinforced by a new concern among historians in 'developed' countries, especially the United States, seeking the origins of modern problems of race relations or of economic inequality between nations. In these ways much new research and many new perspectives have resulted, although gaps and imbalances in knowledge remain and will be reflected in this survey. The very heavy emphasis on sugar is not quite fully justified by its undoubted local importance, and comes partly from the commodity's 'metropolitan' interest. Moreover the great number and variety of small territories has to some extent inhibited generalisation and synthesis. Thus differences in approach have often remained implicit in the literature without generating much open debate or making possible any firm conclusions. But the region's diversity provides unique opportunities for comparative analysis, and a fascinating laboratory in which to investigate problems that affect many other parts of the Third World.

2 The Last Years of Slavery

(i) The colonies of the northern Europeans

For the years preceding slave emancipation much historical discussion focuses upon the economic difficulties of the British, French, Dutch and Danish colonies in the Caribbean. During the seventeenth and eighteenth centuries they had become largely devoted to sugar planting, and had dominated the market for sugar and its by-products in Europe and North America, but their ascendancy was the result of special and temporary circumstances. Most of the territories were small islands, easily served by ocean shipping, a point of great advantage at a time when overland transport was still relatively unimproved. They also benefited from the restrictive colonial policies of Spain and Portugal, which inhibited the development of potentially much more productive American territories. The colonies of each nation had exclusive access to their metropolitan market where, at least in the case of the British, demand for sugar tended to run ahead of supply, thus inflating its price. Furthermore, surviving producers everywhere stood to gain from the slave rebellion of the 1790s in the French colony of St. Domingue (afterwards Haiti), which eliminated a most formidable rival. Certainly there were times of adversity, most commonly the result of international conflicts. For example, the British islands suffered from the mother country's military setbacks during the American War of Independence (1776–82), while they profited from her naval ascendancy through most of the Revolutionary and Napoleonic Wars (1791–1815), to some extent at the expense of their neighbours. But it is clear that sugar planting usually flourished in the colonies of the northern Europeans. After 1815, however, their position was severely affected by the growth of alternative sources of supply. Sugar exports from Brazil, a Portuguese colony until its independence in 1825, and from the Spanish islands of Cuba and Puerto Rico, were stimulated by more liberal government and the high prices which prevailed for some time after

17

the revolution in St. Domingue. During the Napoleonic wars Great Britain had acquired some highly productive new colonies, most notably Trinidad and British Guiana, which developed rapidly as sugar producers. Sugar beet, an innovation promoted by the wartime scarcities, began to be grown extensively in continental Europe. For all of these reasons the price of sugar fell sharply (see Graph, p. 9).

Some earlier studies have identified the American War of Independence as the turning point in the fortunes of the British West Indies [37; 32: 156–78], but now the watershed is usually located in this marked price fall around 1815 [30: 18; 33]. Otherwise, there has been no real dispute about the deteriorating circumstances of the longer-established Caribbean sugar producers. Instead, the main area of doubt concerns the planters' performance and state of morale in conditions of adversity. Some writers have taken an almost wholly unfavourable view, arguing that most of the older colonies were reduced to virtual bankruptcy, while others claim to have detected some evidence of resilience or flexibility. Originally much of the interest in this subject was generated by debate over the significance of the nineteenth-century slave emancipations as episodes in the history of the European colonial powers (see below), but the problem also affects our general understanding of slave-based economies, and of the capacity of the Caribbean plantations to survive the transition from slavery. We will begin with the most pessimistic assessments and then consider the qualifications that have been entered against them.

Ragatz, Williams and others [37; 9: 280–92], have argued that for various reasons the efficiency of West Indian plantations declined as time passed, so that by the early nineteenth century most of the older producers were incapable of adapting to more competitive conditions. The main colonies had been developed in an early phase of intense speculative excitement, during which they had become almost wholly committed to sugar growing. The damaging biological effects of this monoculture – soil exhaustion and plant diseases – were aggravated by widespread absentee ownership, which is believed to have encouraged wasteful and destructive methods of production. Many planters in the West Indies were anxious to make their fortunes and leave as quickly as possible; back in Europe they were unable to supervise effectively the managers left in charge of their property, men who were often ignorant, inexperienced and dishonest. Also many planters ran into debt. This became particularly damaging after 1815 when sugar prices fell much more sharply than interest rates, and loan charges which had been tolerable in the past practically swallowed up any remaining profits. Thus the planters lost their freedom of manoeuvre just when they needed it most. Even if they could escape bankruptcy for a while, their creditors, often the merchants to whom sugar was consigned, were unlikely to tolerate experiments with new crops or equipment which might interrupt production, threaten the security of existing loans, and even require new ones.

It is also alleged that the planters' difficulties were compounded by their almost exclusive reliance upon slave labour. Because the slaves were degraded and brutalised, they were suitable only for the simplest tasks and the most primitive agriculture. So whether or not a planter was indebted or was an absentee, he was unable to offset the natural disadvantages of 'old' land in competition with the 'new' by technical improvements, such as crop rotations or the substitution of the plough for the hoe [58: 51–2; 60: 22]. By the early nineteenth century slavery was a source of weakness also because the institution itself was coming under political attack within Europe, although the precise significance of this movement has been the subject of much debate. Some historians consider that the main source of European anti-slavery feeling was the spread of new moral values [26: 307–8]. Others, of whom Williams has been the most forceful, see hostility to slavery essentially as a response by metropolitan opinion to the autonomous decline of the plantation economy, expressing a desire to liquidate enterprises that had lost their practical usefulness. Hence anti-slavery was a consequence rather than a cause of developments within the West Indies [40]. But recently Williams's interpretation has been viewed with some scepticism [26; 33], and it is widely agreed that the evolution of European opinion, although probably influenced by developments across the Atlantic, had a momentum of its own which helped to reduce confidence in the plantations. Prohibitions on the import of slaves from Africa, the first great achievement of the anti-slavery cause, were made effective for the Danish colonies in 1803, for the British in 1808, for the Dutch in 1826, and for the French in 1831. The usual outcomes were decreases in both slave populations and the output of sugar [9: 280; 23: 125; 41: 48–9]. From 1823 British governments were committed to the principle of emancipation, and once the final decision had been taken in 1833 to implement it, other colonial powers could be expected to follow.

So, it has been argued, with all these forces working against them, the traditional sugar colonies were in a state of acute and perhaps terminal crisis after 1815 [32: *186–207*; 50: *7–32*]. However, a number of objections can be made to this pessimistic diagnosis. Its original and most uncompromising exponents relied heavily on information published at the time (until recently all that was available in any quantity), especially the loud complaints of economic distress coming from the planters themselves, or the strictures of the anti-slavery campaigners; for obvious reasons evidence of this kind cannot be accepted uncritically. As historians have gained access to a wider range of source materials, including the private papers of estates, they have qualified some earlier judgements. Cases have come to light of planters who took an interest in technical improvement, despite slavery and absentee ownership [36: *103–40*; 32: *167–73*; 57]. Also, the assertion that the continuous production of sugar must lead almost inevitably to soil exhaustion, with 'new' land displacing the 'old', has little basis in either biological or historical fact: sugar cane is distinguished among tropical crops for its capacity to conserve the land upon which it grows [74: *15*], and some of the earliest 'monocultural' islands – Barbados in particular [20] – have proved most resilient over the long term. Thus the stagnation or decline of sugar production in the older colonies, and even the liquidation of individual estates, may reflect not a wholesale bankruptcy but the elimination of some marginal operations brought into being by protected markets and high prices, which could not hope to survive as conditions became more competitive [14: *247*; 58: *46*]. Yet how many of the sugar estates were inevitably doomed, and how many might be expected to continue? It is easy to answer a question of this kind with sweeping generalisation, but difficult to arrive at a firmly established conclusion. Here we can only mention some of the main lines of inquiry.

If the planters' public assertions of their own misfortune are untrustworthy, what is the evidence of their private records? Several plantation archives have now been examined which seem to indicate that some financial strength remained even after 1815. Rates of return on capital certainly fell from previous levels, but profits still appear in the accounts more frequently than losses [20:

102; 13: 77, 398–406, 454–5; 30: 174–5; 27; 39; 41: 168–71].
However, only a very small proportion of estates have left records, and those from a minority of especially favoured properties may have had better than average chances of survival. So it is doubtful whether argument from particular instances can ever be conclusive. Only one published attempt, by Eisner for Jamaica in 1832[14: 26], has been made to calculate profitability for a whole colony. She also suggests that significant profits were still being made, but this part of her work does not seem to have had much influence. In any case, sugar planting must be assessed in the context of contemporary expectations. Perhaps it was still profitable, but at a rate so low as to be inadequate for such a precarious activity, vulnerable to drought, hurricane, naval blockade or slave rebellion. These were the terms in which eighteenth-century planters had justified their relatively high incomes. But how far were the great fortunes made in the earlier period a reasonable compensation for risk, and how far the result of monopoly power in the sugar market? Monopoly rents might be eliminated by the growth of competition after 1815 to leave returns that, although reduced, were still sufficiently attractive to investors, despite their complaints, particularly considering that there may have been a shortage of alternative outlets for capital by the 1820s [29: 197–8]. Of course the declining profits and sugar prices were themselves a new source of insecurity, but it is not clear whether they appeared as a trend that was likely to continue indefinitely, as a permanent adjustment to post-war conditions, or as a temporary and reversible depression. Curtin notices that the Jamaican planters had recovered from earlier crises and they might hope to do so again [55: 6–7].

One possible guide to the planters' feelings is their attitude towards slave ownership. If the estates had become generally unprofitable, or insufficiently profitable, then it might be expected that many slaves would have been freed voluntarily by their masters. In fact wholesale manumissions were rare, and the main examples come not from sugar colonies but from the much less important cotton-growing areas, such as the Bahamas or the Coronie district of Surinam, which were severely affected by soil erosion and competition from the United States [23: 227; 58: 105]. On the other hand, planters may have held on to their slaves not because they were profitable but from fear of public disorder if they were freed, for reasons of social prestige, or for the sake of the compensation payments that were to be expected when general emancipation was decreed by the colonial power, as Goslinga claims in the case of Surinam [15: *157–8*]. Indeed it has been implied that some slave owners, especially absentees, privately welcomed compensated emancipation as a convenient release [36: *316–19*], but once again the evidence is ambiguous. The planters' public reaction to proposals that slavery be ended was usually one of virulent hostility, although it often included a demand for compensation if the decision should go against them. So did they emphasise their rights as slave owners in order to secure generous compensation? Or did they emphasise their claims for compensation as a defence of slavery, to remind their opponents of the costs that any interference with the principle of private property might entail? The few public conversions of slave holders to the principle of emancipation, among Jamaican proprietors in 1832, or those of Guadeloupe in 1847, come very late and may reflect an acceptance of overwhelming political realities rather than calculations of economic advantage [35: *231*; 41: *158*].

Another way of measuring West Indian prospects is to seek more specific information about investment behaviour. Those who take a pessimistic view argue that as a result of a general loss of confidence, the plantations' capital equipment was allowed to deteriorate, or at least it was not improved sufficiently to keep them abreast of their new competitors. Once again there is a good deal of conflicting evidence. Thus, while Green, Craton and Walvin mention estates where investment was neglected [32: *186–8*; 58: *44*], Pares and Checkland offer counter-examples where it was maintained or even increased [29: *194–9*; 36: *301*]. And whatever level of investment may have been achieved, there is still the problem of deciding how appropriate it was in the circumstances. Craton, Williams and others claim that technological progress in the older colonies was hamstrung by low profitability, the scarcity of investible funds, and absentee ownership [9: *369*; 30: *155*]. Yet Boogaart and Emmer, for example, report that between 1816 and 1860 two-thirds of Surinam's sugar estates were supplied with steam engines [25: *223*]. This could be seen as a creditable performance given the cost and unreliability of steam power in its early stages. Again, Adamson cites, as evidence of the British West Indies' moribund state under slavery, the failure of planters to introduce the vacuum pan for sugar boiling, invented in 1813 and to become of great importance later in the century [50: 27]. According to Deerr [2: II, 559], this invention was 'one of the few and exceptional instances of a master patent appearing and being successful from its inception'. Le Riverend Brusone, however, believes it was too costly in its original form [16: 355] and Checkland draws on the experience of the Gladstone estates to emphasise the engineering difficulties that had to be solved before it could work efficiently [29: 266]. Moreover, both Green and Adamson have argued that even when this had been accomplished, its introduction was made uneconomic for the time being by the structure of British sugar duties [58: 453; 50: 173]. In short, the economics of early nineteenth-century sugar technology have not yet been studied in sufficient detail for it to be possible to discriminate with any confidence between such alternatives.

One special aspect of the problem of plantation capital that has attracted much attention is slave demography. In the eighteenth century the harsh conditions of the sugar estates had caused a persistent excess of deaths over births among the slaves, and their numbers were maintained only by purchase from Africa. After the early nineteenth-century prohibitions of trans-Atlantic slave trading this was no longer possible, and so attempts were made to secure natural increase by better standards of maintenance and reduced work loads, with very uncertain results [34]. In every sugar colony except Barbados slave numbers fell after the end of the trade from Africa. But when this fact was cited against the planters as evidence that their attempts at 'Amelioration' were ineffective, they often argued that the trend was only temporary: the last generations of imported Africans would die out, to leave only locally-born slaves ('Creoles'[3]) with rather better rates of natural reproduction, and then populations would stabilise or even increase. Perhaps there was some truth in these claims, for slave deaths were nearly matched by births in the British Leeward Islands and Jamaica by the 1820s, and in the French islands by the 1840s, although substantial excess mortality continued in British Guiana, Surinam and St. Croix [35: 136; 41: 48–57; 23: 170; 13: 463]. But even where demographic equilibrium was reached, it is not clear that this could be seen as securing the estates' long-term viability. Publicly at least, the planters asserted that without access to the slave trade they incurred heavy extra costs in more generous maintenance, and in the greater proportion of slaves who, as breeding women or children, were incapable of work. So they would be unable to compete with Cuba or Brazil where the import of new slaves, mostly productive young adults, was still permitted. Sheridan has examined these claims and found them to be substantially correct [38]. On the other hand Bennett's study of one property in Barbados suggests that Amelioration could be an economic success, with its incidental costs offset by the improving quality of the labour force and the ending of outlays for new slaves [28: *136–41*].

Recent investigations of early nineteenth-century Jamaica by Higman and by Craton have taken a different approach in emphasising some wider aspects of the adjustments taking place on the estates which may be important for our understanding, not just of the position and morale of the planters, but also of the slaves' attitudes and their behaviour after emancipation. Higman argues that although there was little technical innovation, some flexibility in estate management could be achieved by concentrating slaves into units closer to the optimum size, diversifying into 'minor staples' such as ginger and pimento, or ending the customary exemption of coloured (mixed race) slaves from field work. In these ways efficiency was maintained despite the changes in the slave population that followed the end of the African trade, and despite the measures taken to encourage breeding. Certainly the market value of output fell sharply, but this was the result of depressed prices, not of insoluble economic problems within the plantations, and some profits apparently remained for their owners [35: *212–32*]. In Higman's view the final overthrow of slavery in Jamaica (and by extension in the rest of the British West Indies), was the result of changes in social relations, although much of their effect may have come from the fact that they operated upon an institution whose economic position was weak. So long as the slave trade continued, Africans had usually been put to field work, while a large proportion of the creole men could expect some kind of privileged occupation. But from 1808 this was no longer possible and many Creoles failed to secure the promotion that they had come to expect. Their disappointment contributed to the Jamaican slave rebellion of 1831, which finally persuaded metropolitan opinion to introduce emancipation [35: *210–11, 227–32*].

Craton also detects an accumulation of social tensions, while representing the underlying economic situation in darker terms: the plantations faced a 'catastrophic decline', which meant more work and reduced allowances for many slaves. In this context he considers any ameliorating measures to have been nugatory, and is sceptical whether there was much demographic improvement on the sugar estates [31: *109*; 30: *86, 97, 131, 139*]. Apart from these material pressures, and the Creoles' frustrated hopes for promotion, Craton also notes the aspiration of many slaves for greater opportunities to cultivate independently the plots of land which they had often been allowed for their maintenance. So he interprets the Jamaican rebellion and similar episodes in Barbados and British Guiana as 'proto-peasant revolts' [31].

Such emphasis upon developments within the plantations as a cause of unrest is rather novel. It has long been recognised that slave rebellions became more frequent in the nineteenth century throughout the Caribbean (providing another reason why the planters' self-confidence declined). But growing unrest has been usually interpreted as the result of external influences, in particular of reports from Europe on the progress of political radicalism and the anti-slavery movement [9: *320–7*; 58: *125*]. At the moment it is probably impossible to decide conclusively between these alternative views. Higman's and Craton's conclusions are backed by a thoroughness in research hitherto unmatched in studies of Caribbean slavery, but difficulties remain with the detail of their argument. For example, they are unable to establish any clear increase in the frequency of running away, the only form of slave resistance apart from collective rebellion for which there is useful information [30: *186*; 35: *178–83*]. Yet an increase might have been expected if estate populations were being progressively alienated by long-term social forces. And their findings have not yet been adequately confirmed outside Jamaica, so even if they have local validity, perhaps they cannot be safely extended to other colonies. Recent studies of Guadeloupe by Schnakenbourg [41: *104–18*], of St. Croix by Degn [13: *482–91*], and of Cuba by Scott [45: *86, 108–9*], still attribute the growth of slave resistance mainly to external or political influences.

(ii) CUBA AND PUERTO RICO

So far we have concentrated upon the colonies of the northern European nations in the years before slave emancipation, and our task has been to evaluate what was clearly a phase of economic depression. The case of the Spanish islands, Cuba and Puerto Rico, is different, for here sugar production increased through most of the nineteenth century (see Table II). The main reasons for this relative success are generally agreed: a change to more liberal government policies, superior natural resources, the more general introduction of improved techniques, and a late continuation of the slave trade, to Puerto Rico on a substantial scale until the 1840s, and to Cuba until the 1850s [25: 558; 48: 638]. Therefore most discussion has concerned the character of Spanish Caribbean slavery and the reasons why it was eventually abolished, in Puerto Rico during the 1870s and in Cuba during the 1880s.

While for the rest of the region it may be plausible to interpret emancipation as at least in part a response to protracted economic decline, clearly this cannot be very convincing for the Spanish islands. Some writers, however, believe that economic forces were decisive in bringing an end to slavery here too, although they operated in another way. According to Moreno Fraginals's study of Cuba, from the 1840s sugar planters were investing heavily in steam engines and other elaborate equipment for processing the cane. These required more skill from their operators than the traditional techniques and were beyond the capacity of the degraded slave population. So planters turned increasingly to alternative sources of labour – locally-born freemen, immigrant Europeans, and workers brought under contract from China – and slavery came to be seen as inefficient and anachronistic. Thus its abolition, although formally imposed from Spain, enjoyed a good deal of support from the local elite, in contrast to the colonies of the northern Europeans, where emancipation was much more obviously the result of changes in metropolitan opinion [44; 22: 184–9].

Other historians, while accepting that slavery was unhelpful to technical modernisation, are reluctant to give quite as much prominence to economic considerations in the movement for emancipation. Knight describes how in Cuba the issue was influenced by the desire for independence from Spain, by fears of slave rebellion and changes in the island's racial composition, and by the example of slave emancipation in the United States in 1865 [43: 137–78]. Scott has carried her dissent further, by doubting whether there was any fundamental incompatibility between slavery and the new technology, and by pointing out that slaves were employed with steam engines and vacuum pans in the most advanced mills [45: 89, 94–5]. Other writers have noticed how Puerto Rican planters commonly

Table II
Average Annual Sugar Production ('000 tons)

	British West Indies	French West Indies	Cuba	Puerto Rico	Dominican Republic	Total Caribbean	Rest of world Cane	Rest of world Beet	Total world
1820–9	185	53	57	10	—	331	n.a.	n.a.	n.a.
1830–9	190	54	131	25	—	427	n.a.	n.a.	n.a.
1840–9	136	55	192	40	—	449	500	67	1 016
1850–9	162	46	345	45	—	620	624	259	1 503
1860–9	207	58	580	55	—	920	571	579	2 070
1870–9	247	81	645	83	2	1 074	731	1 242	3 047
1880–9	284	87	595	73	10	1 069	1 283	2 505	4 857
1890–9	260	72	638	57	35	1 076	1 990	4 292	7 358
1900–9	244	70	1 655	173	58	2 217	4 290	7 020	13 527
1910–19	246	65	2 647	375	119	3 469	6 738	6 693	16 900
1920–9	312	59	4 335	514	277	5 523	9 134	7 429	22 086
1930–9	485	89	2 842	844	415	4 731	12 119	10 084	26 934
1940–9	637	99	3 957	914	502	6 164	9 836	8 160	24 160
1950–9	1 028	172	5 367	1 041	703	8 375	14 768	15 325	38 468
1960–9	1 255	235	5 389	802	817	8 569	25 516	26 222	60 307

Sources: [2; 22: 1560–4; 95: 71, 147; 74: 112–13].

27

preferred to give training in processing work to their slaves, over whom they had full control, while hiring free men to help with the less skilled field tasks [6: *110–11*; 25: *561*]. The sharp rise in the price of Cuban slaves during the 1850s and 1860s perhaps indicates that they were still highly valued as workers, although more difficult to obtain because of growing restrictions on the trade from Africa. Other types of labour may have been introduced, not for any intrinsic advantages in mechanised production, but simply because the supply of new slaves had been so drastically curtailed [48: *638–9*; 45: *99*]. In this sense external rather than internal pressures were decisive in bringing Spanish Caribbean slavery to an end. The main difficulty in judging these points is a scarcity of detailed information on developments at the level of the individual estate, and a tendency in some existing accounts to rely upon aggregate or circumstantial evidence, much of it rather ambiguous. For example, the rising Cuban slave prices can be construed more as a symptom of demographic crisis and a source of uncertainty, rather than as indicating that slave ownership was still considered a reasonably attractive proposition [16: *339*]. We do not really know how matters were perceived by the majority of planters. The expressions of discontent with slavery cited by Moreno Fraginals were mostly from liberal publicists, not necessarily representative in their opinions [44: *135, 141*; 43: *139*].

However one point is clear: before slavery was abolished planters in Cuba and Puerto Rico had begun, for whatever reasons, to experiment with alternative forms of labour, and in this they were quite distinctive. As Adamson puts it for the British West Indies, planters there 'could no more conceive of growing sugar without slaves than they could of making it themselves' [50: *26*]. Such relative flexibility seems to have helped Spanish Caribbean planters to accept emancipation with better grace than their counterparts elsewhere in the region, and adjust more successfully to its aftermath. Perhaps all this was due principally to their greater economic strength and the advantages in technical innovation that it gave (see below p. 38). But influence may also have been exerted by the character of Spanish colonial slavery, which some writers suggest was less harsh than elsewhere in the Americas, because of regulation by metropolitan authorities and the influence of the Catholic church. Klein has applied this hypothesis at length to Cuba [42], and other historians, in a rather more casual way, postulate international differences between Caribbean slave regimes, with a spectrum of severity increasing from the Spanish colonies, through those of the French and the British, to the Dutch in Surinam as possibly the worst case [11: 26; 23: 131; 54: 70, 78].

However this kind of argument has rather fallen into disrepute. Much of it is based upon weakly enforced official provisions for the treatment of slaves. Knight and others [43: 59–84; 44: 142–3; 22: 174–83] have presented evidence that Cuban slaves experienced relatively mild conditions only while they were employed in the towns or the less arduous types of agriculture, as was usually the case until the late eighteenth century. Their situation on the sugar plantations that subsequently developed so rapidly was as bad as anywhere else in the Caribbean, a point which Klein partly concedes [42: 150–8]. Thus economics rather than national culture were the decisive influence on the slaves' material condition. Nevertheless, although we can probably take this as conclusively established, the Spanish islands certainly had been remarkable among their neighbours for unusually high rates of manumission and white immigration, perhaps mainly as a result of the rather modest share of sugar planting in their economies. Before emancipation, slaves made up only about 7 per cent of Puerto Rico's population and 28 per cent of Cuba's, while the corresponding proportion for the French West Indies was 75 per cent and for the British West Indies 85 per cent [5: 238–9; 43: 86]. Whether a cause or effect of these variations, racial attitudes in the Spanish colonies do not seem to have been quite so rigid as in other Caribbean plantation societies and the stigma attaching to sugar as 'slave work', while certainly present, seems to have been less pronounced [6: 82–130; 43: 179–94]. This may have helped planters in their efforts at adaptation. Certainly Knight and Moreno Fraginals imply that in Cuba any erosion of racial barriers within the sugar industry was essentially a consequence of technical change and the growing need for skilled manpower, which 'under the prevailing circumstances, had to be white' [43: 182; 44: 131–42]. But there is evidence that unskilled white labour could be incorporated even before extensive mechanisation had begun [44: 41, 131; 16: 334–7].

(iii) CONCLUSION

Despite considerable local differences, and uncertainties on points of detail, recent research both on the Spanish islands and the other Caribbean colonies has convincingly identified a measure of adaptability in slavery on the plantations during the years immediately before emancipation [28; 35; 45; 57]. This modifies earlier interpretations, derived originally from the nineteenth-century critics of slavery, according to which the institution had become completely unviable as technical change accelerated and international trade was liberalised [37; 44]. In the evolution of historiography on this point there are similarities between the Caribbean and the United States. Over the last 30 years established opinion has been reversed by the accumulation of evidence that plantation slavery in the southern USA remained profitable and dynamic up to the outbreak of the Civil War in 1860 [46]. However the analogy between the two regions should not be pushed too far, because the southern United States had certain special advantages. Demand for cotton, its main product, was growing more rapidly than for the sugar exports of the Caribbean. As part of a single national state with an expanding western frontier, its planters had greater opportunities for moving their slaves to better soils on larger and more efficient units of production. Finally, the slave population of the United States had by the nineteenth century achieved natural increase, with a regular excess of births over deaths, so curtailment of the trade from Africa did not have such alarming long-term implications as in the Caribbean [34: 266–8]. For all these reasons it is likely that while North American planters remained generally prosperous during the last years of slavery, among their counterparts in the Caribbean there was a more complicated mixture of successful adjustment and severe adversity, which will always be more difficult to evaluate.

3   Adjustments to Emancipation

Slavery was ended throughout the Caribbean during the nineteenth century, at different times in the different territories.[4] In Haiti and the Dominican Republic the change was achieved by local action; otherwise it was managed more or less by the colonial power, usually with some compensation to former slave owners by the use of monetary payments and periods of regulated labour, such as 'apprenticeship' in the British West Indies (1834–8), or the *patrona-to* in Cuba (1880–6) [58: *129–61*; 69]. As the main function of slavery had been to support sugar planting, the most convenient measure of the results of emancipation is the subsequent history of sugar production, and from the information on this point summarised in Table III it will be seen that there were considerable local variations. In Haiti sugar planting was soon virtually eliminated; elsewhere there was a more gradual but persistent decline, or a recovery (sometimes only temporary) after early post-emancipation difficulties, while in a few cases output grew without serious interruption.

These tendencies were closely associated with wider developments in economic structure. In general, to the extent that sugar production was sustained, the plantations remained intact and dominant; to the extent that it failed, they lost ground to small-scale agriculture. These consequences are still felt today. At one extreme is Haiti, where the estates have been almost completely displaced by peasant farmers; at the other is St. Kitts where more than 90 per cent of the cultivated area is occupied by plantations; while Jamaica, for example, falls in between with large holdings controlling 56 per cent of its farm land in 1961 [1: *193, 258–9, 321*]. There are some complicating influences. Large estates might survive without sugar, by raising cattle or crops such as bananas, coffee or cocoa. In colonies like Trinidad that were particularly well endowed with fertile, unoccupied land at the time of emancipation, a peasantry could develop alongside a strong plantation economy. Also by the later nineteenth century developments in processing technology

31

made it economic to grow sugar cane on small farms [48: *655–7*; *79*: *116–17*]. As a rule, however, peasantries and plantations were in competition: where one was strong the other was weak, and the plantations' strength depended mainly upon sugar. So the purpose of this chapter is to consider why sugar planting adjusted more successfully to emancipation in some colonies than in others. Four main lines of inquiry have been pursued on this subject: (i) the ratio of population to land area; (ii) the plantations' profitability and efficiency; (iii) political opportunities for the coercion of 'free' labour; and (iv) the character of social relations. No author has concentrated exclusively on any one of these points; it is generally agreed that the pattern of adjustment was determined by a variety of forces and the problem is to estimate their relative importance. But on the whole those historians who are most strongly convinced that the sugar plantations have been inherently exploitative, and damaging to the general economic development of the Caribbean, go furthest in emphasising points (i) and (iii).

(i) THE RATIO OF POPULATION TO LAND AREA

It is commonly assumed that most ex-slaves had developed a strong aversion to plantation life and sought to escape it wherever possible, usually by establishing themselves as independent cultivators. They may still have intended to work for the estates occasionally, earning cash to supplement their incomes from other activities, but attendance on these terms was unreliable and impaired the efficiency of sugar production. So unless estate owners could find some alternative source of labour, the plantations were likely to be severely weakened through the establishment of peasant farms by ex-slaves. This happened most readily in the more sparsely populated colonies, where there were substantial reserves of land on which the former slaves could settle, subject to various legal and institutional constraints (see below, pp. 40–1). Conversely the plantations' chances of uninterrupted prosperity were greatest when the ratio of population to land area was relatively high. Table III gives empirical support to this argument. After emancipation sugar production increased in 'high-density' colonies such as Barbados, St. Kitts or Antigua, but often fell in conditions of 'low density'. So it is widely believed that the ratio of land area to population was the most powerful single influence on the estates' chances of survival,

32

especially in the British West Indies [58: *192–5*; 56: *196–200*].

However, while there is an obvious association between population density and the course of sugar production, it is by no means complete, even among the British colonies. For example, output in St. Lucia, Dominica or Trinidad was maintained rather more successfully than in Montserrat or St. Vincent. To some extent matters are confused by local peculiarities: the quality of land varied between colonies, the continental interior of British Guiana and Surinam was virtually inaccessible, and the Spanish islands had by Caribbean standards unusually large numbers of resident white proprietors. So the ratio of land area to population is not an exact measure of the ex-slaves' chances of gaining independence as peasant farmers. However, even allowing for such complications, population density at the time of emancipation remains a rather erratic guide to the estates' subsequent fortunes. A further problem is the possibility of migration. Barbados, St. Kitts and Antigua were within a few days' sailing distance of colonies where land was abundant, so why should their freedmen not have taken advantage of this opportunity? Some writers emphasise the legal restraints on mobility secured by planters anxious to protect their supplies of labour [50: *44*], but the British Colonial Office did not allow any outright prohibition of movement between colonies, and Hall, Richardson and Levy consider that the ex-slaves had some freedom to migrate [60: *41–8*; 65; 63: *80–3*]. All this suggests that other influences apart from population density may have been significant.

(ii) THE PLANTATIONS' PROFITABILITY AND EFFICIENCY

If the survival of the plantations was not determined solely by their ex-slaves' access to land then other explanations must be considered. For example it may have been necessary and possible for estates to attract labour from alternative occupations through the wages and conditions of employment that they offered. These were determined fundamentally by levels of profitability and efficiency. This was the argument of some contemporary liberals who had predicted that as free workers were naturally more productive than slaves, the plantations should benefit from emancipation. If they did not, the reason must have been their pre-emancipation decadence. It was alleged that some hard-pressed owners simply abandoned their estates during the first years of freedom, while many of

33

Table III
Land-Population Ratios and Changes in Sugar Production after Emancipation

British Colonies	(1) Land-population ratio (square miles per thousand total population at emancipation)	(2) Percentage change in average annual sugar production after emancipation[a]	(3) Period in which pre-emancipation level of sugar production regained
Barbados	1.7	+6	1834–
St. Kitts	2.9	+4	1839–
Antigua	3.1	+9	1834–
Montserrat	4.6	−44	1866–96
Nevis	5.0	−43	1871–82
St. Vincent	5.7	−47	never
Grenada	6.3	−56	never
Tobago	8.8	−48	never

Jamaica	12.2	−51	1934–
St. Lucia	15.5	−22	1858–
Dominica	16.3	−6	1842–89
Trinidad	47.7	+22	1834–
British Guiana	832.4	−43	1861–
Other Territories			
Haiti	20.6	−95	never
Martinique	3.3	−30	1859–
Guadeloupe	5.1	−45	1870–
Surinam	1 000.0	−38	1927–31
Puerto Rico	4.7	−21	1902–
Cuba	26.2	+25	1885–

[a] For the British colonies, between the periods 1824–33 and 1839–46; for other territories, between the 5 years before and the 5 years after emancipation, excluding any intervening phase of restricted freedom.

Sources: [56: 196, 202; 2; 5: 239–41; 17: 65, 84–6].

those who survived could only offer employment that was arduous, poorly paid and irregular. Thus the ex-slaves who withdrew to become peasant farmers were making a rational choice of the economically more rewarding activity. Conversely, a plantation that was reasonably productive ought to be able to recruit labour and survive, even in an area of low population density. A number of historians have followed this line of reasoning to a certain extent [14: *192*; 79: *105–6*].

The argument must turn on two points: first, the economic condition of the estates – what standards of employment did they provide? – and second, the attitudes and aspirations of the ex-slaves – how responsive were they likely to have been to any economic inducements that the estates could offer? We have already seen that there is disagreement on the first question for the years preceding emancipation, and this extends to its aftermath. According to Goslinga, when Surinam's slaves had been emancipated in 1863, 'after cashing their compensation, most of the planters sold their plantations and liquidated their business .... There were a few courageous and optimistic men whose money did not leave the colony but who invested in the development of their land, but these were in the minority' [15: *158*]. Van Lier, on the other hand, implies that there was a greater proportion of optimists in Surinam [23: *183–4*]. It is sometimes said that much of the Jamaican plantation economy was on the point of bankruptcy by 1834 [32: *185–90*], yet detailed studies by Hall and Green suggest that many planters tried hard to continue the production of sugar at least until 1846, when the loss of tariff protection in the British market brought a sharp reduction in its price [57: *205–11*; 59: *37–65, 100–19*]. In general it seems that the wholesale abandonment of sugar planting as an immediate response to emancipation was not very common, outside a few obviously marginal areas, such as the British Virgin Islands. But it is clear that many estates were maintained for a few years only under conditions of great uncertainty and stress, so quite possibly it was their poor terms of employment that prevented them from recruiting an adequate labour force. This was strenuously denied by the planters who argued that the real problem was the ex-slaves' insufficient 'civilisation'. In a tropical climate, with abundant land, basic subsistence was easily secured, and the freedmen's 'artificial wants' were so limited that no wage could induce an adequate supply of labour: the higher the rate of pay, the less they would work.

Some historians have accepted this view, while expressing it more sympathetically. According to Kloosterboer, after emancipation 'the Negroes did not feel much inclined to work, and especially not on the plantations since to their minds slave-driving was an inherent factor in such labour' [49: 4]. Alternatively Mintz has seen the freedmen as highly industrious and acquisitive, but determined wherever possible to reinforce their separate identity away from the estates, continuing the tradition of small-scale production and marketing that had been established in most 'low-density' areas under slavery [6: 131–250]. 'Thus Caribbean peasantries represent a *mode of response* to the plantation system and its connotations, and a *mode of resistance* to imposed styles of life' [6: 132–3]. Many historians have found this approach useful; for example, it plays an important part in Craton's analysis of the late slave rebellions (see above, p. 25). However in most recent discussions, including Mintz's [24: 222], the antagonism between plantations and the peasant way of life is presented rather less emphatically. For the British West Indies Craton believes that the rebel slaves wanted the sugar estates to survive, since plantations would provide them with the chance of occasional wage work [31: 118–21]. Hall argues that 'the movement of the ex-slaves from the estates in the immediate post-emancipation years was not a flight from the horrors of slavery. It was a protest against the inequities of early "freedom"', for example the planters' clumsy attempts to discipline their workers by denying them the customary free use of houses and provision grounds [61: 23]. According to Marshall, 'ex-slaves had more of an interest in improving their standard of living than in seeking "independence"' [24: 246].

Former slaves, therefore, may have been more pragmatic, more susceptible to variations in wages and conditions than Mintz's original argument implied. Thus in the British Leeward Islands population density was lowest, and opportunities for independent cultivation were greatest, on Nevis and Montserrat. These two islands also suffered heavy falls in sugar production after emancipation (see Table III), but apparently not just because of labour shortages resulting from the development of a peasantry, for local wage rates were exceptionally low [66: 29]. An important influence was the very weak position of their estates, a consequence of difficult terrain and poor methods, and many ex-slaves reacted by seeking temporary work on plantations elsewhere [60: 41, 50–5; 65]. When in the 1860s some technical innovations temporarily improved the islands' competitive position and allowed the payment of higher wages, emigration was reduced and sugar production increased [2:*1, 195–6*; 79: *43*].

Adjustment to emancipation may sometimes have been eased by contemporary developments in the processing of cane into exportable sugar, through the use of larger steam-powered mills and the vacuum pan. The continuing failure of the British West Indies during the 1830s and 1840s to make progress in this area has been emphasised, and taken as evidence of their often hopeless condition, with estates too small and unproductive to accommodate the improvements, and too entangled with debts to amalgamate [58: *210–13*; 59: *100–7*]. Even so, as in the period before emancipation (see above, pp. 22–3), it is difficult to judge what rate of innovation would have been appropriate. But it is clear that the plantations on many islands where emancipation came later benefited from a more rapid diffusion of the new technology, perhaps because of its progressive refinement, or other favourable influences. Central factories, receiving cane grown on estates which had given up processing, were first built on Guadeloupe and Martinique just before the slaves were freed in 1848, and dealt with most of the crop on these islands by the 1880s, when sugar production substantially exceeded pre-emancipation levels. Progress may have been easier than in the British colonies because of previous French experience with beet sugar (an important source of innovations for the processing of cane), a lower level of indebtedness to outside merchants, and a metropolitan government more willing to provide direct support for planting interests, especially through the fostering of banks [2: *1, 235–6*; 79: *81–6*; 12: *227–44*]. Central factories also became important soon after emancipation in St. Croix and Cuba [2: *245*; 13: *499–509*; 22: *271–80*]. Sugar industries reformed in this way were more likely to survive: they could afford to pay higher wages and could get by with less labour in proportion to their output.

Yet while greater efficiency may have helped many planters, there are reasons for doubting whether as a general rule it could have been sufficient to recruit the ex-slaves. The estates of British Guiana, a relatively fertile and productive colony, paid some of the highest wages in the British West Indies, yet suffered heavy withdrawals of labour [66: *29*; 50: *34–41*]. Craton shows how one Jamaican estate was unable to get sufficient labour in the 1840s, despite making heavy investments, offering employment throughout the year, and giving up its attempts to charge rents for houses and grounds [30: 281–313]. Also evidence about the ex-slaves' economic aspirations as indicated by their behaviour as peasant cultivators is equivocal. Some authors emphasise their dynamic response to market opportunities [6: 159; 55: 110–12; 59: 157–206], but in Surinam, according to Van Lier, the creole small-holders who settled near Paramaribo, the principal town, made no serious attempt to supply its demand for food [23: 225]. Eisner calculates that in Jamaica per capita production of staple foods for local consumption fell between 1832 and 1850, and the growth in the output of peasant export crops was much less than the decline of sugar [14: 9–11, 263–4; 58: 251–2]. Fallope-Lara reports a similar outcome in Guadeloupe during the 1850s [69: 145–7]. Perhaps many ex-slaves responded to opportunities for a cash income, whether from the estates or their own land, only up to a certain point, because their desire for money and the things it could buy was rather limited. If so, then although individual estates that were more efficient than the average may have had an edge over their neighbours in competition for available supplies of wage labour, it is misleading to argue that they could all have solved their problems simply by raising themselves to the standards of the best.

(iii) POLITICAL OPPORTUNITIES FOR THE COERCION OF 'FREE' LABOUR

Some writers believe that the topics considered so far are of secondary importance because the essence of any plantation system is the exercise of authority by a ruling elite. Adamson introduces his study of post-emancipation British Guiana with this declaration:

> I hope it will become abundantly clear that the continued production of sugar without slaves had nothing to do with the operation of blind economic forces. On the contrary, the survival of sugar was the result of several deliberate acts of policy. [50: 32]

Planters certainly had great political influence, which they sought to exercise in support of their economic interests, especially in securing a labour supply. Their methods included laws of contract and 'vagrancy', and constraints on the acquisition of land by peasant cultivators. Also the small-holding class that did emerge was starved of government support in the provision of schools, roads, and other infrastructure, while being burdened with discriminatory taxes [50: 34–159]. Perhaps the most striking expressions of the planters' power were the officially-sponsored schemes to introduce labour from outside the region. Between the 1830s and the early twentieth century about 800,000 immigrants reached the Caribbean in this way, two-thirds from British India, most of the rest from China and West Africa. Cuba (before emancipation), British Guiana and Trinidad were the main recipients, but significant numbers also went to Surinam, Guadeloupe, Martinique and Jamaica [48: 642]. Usually the imported workers were bound by contract ('indentured') to a particular employer for 5–10 years after their arrival, so they could be disciplined to a degree that many ex-slaves had refused to accept, and it was hoped that their presence as competitors for employment would help to make the Creoles more cooperative. The immigration programmes entailed heavy transport costs, and were extensively subsidised from general taxation [58: 261–93; 50: 104–9].

Evidently such measures were sometimes helpful to the planters, but it has proved difficult to establish their relative importance as influences on the estates' fortunes. For example, in Puerto Rico a series of decrees, culminating in the Ley General de Jornaleros of 1849, stipulated that landless freemen should seek employment from landowners, and Mintz considers that these laws made available an important supplement to slave labour. Although repealed at the time of emancipation in 1873, he argues that they had long-term consequences for the pattern of social relations [6: 82–94]. According to Bergad [95: 116–24] however, they could not be made fully effective while unoccupied land was still available, so perhaps the high density of population reached in Puerto Rico by the later nineteenth century was the main reason why its planters were relatively successful in maintaining their position. In Cuba, which was more sparsely settled, similar attempts at direct coercion do not seem to have achieved very much either before or after emancipation [44: 137]; in Guadeloupe during the 1850s they were vitiated by widespread passive resistance [69: 107–9]; while Green believes that in the British colonies 'contract laws, however rigorous, were largely ineffectual' against freedmen [58: 175]. Also official restraints on the formation of small holdings were not comprehensively applied [14: *347*; 68: *51–2, 86–96*; 51: *442*], and the results of taxation practices are unclear. Some colonists certainly hoped to pressurise the ex-slaves into seeking wage work by raising import duties on items of popular consumption, but any local action may have been offset by the metropolitan measures for the general liberalisation of imperial trade which were fashionable about the middle of the nineteenth century. Thus Levy notices that the British Possessions Act of 1842 substantially lowered prices in Barbados [63: *97–8*]. No comprehensive study has yet been undertaken of Caribbean living costs to clarify the point. And if they were raised by acts of policy, did this have the intended effect of increasing the supply of labour to the estates? Some contemporaries believed that higher import duties would tend to encourage peasant self-sufficiency instead [14: *366*].

Even indentured immigration could not guarantee the planters a solution to their labour problems, for while some writers have likened it to slavery [71: *101*], there were differences – limited terms of service, and official regulation of standards, however erratically enforced – which made it less advantageous to the estate owner than slaves had been, even with subsidies [48: *645–6*]. Immigrants were used extensively only in the most productive colonies, such as British Guiana and Trinidad. Elsewhere prospective employers found contract labour too costly, although in the case of Jamaica it is not clear how far this was a result of the estates' fundamental economic weaknesses, or of the peculiarities in local politics which prevented planters here from acting decisively in their own interests [58: *242–9, 356–68*; 55: *138–40*; 59: *96–107*].

The most obvious test for the economic significance of political coercion is the evolution of labour costs and technology in the territories where coercion was principally applied. As the planters' main aim was to secure a ready supply of workers, we might expect that any success would have been expressed in reduced real wage rates. It is sometimes also argued that they were able to rely on 'cheap labour' rather than technical improvements to maintain the viability of their estates, and that their measures were very damaging to other local activities. According to Mintz, the arrival of indentured immigrants in the Caribbean 'was immensely important in shoring up an ... archaic sugar technology, while obstructing peasant development in those same societies' [6: *215*]. For such

41

reasons economies in which plantation interests were dominant are believed to have experienced low rates of growth in efficiency and per capita income [50: 19; 76: 42–8].

A certain amount of evidence on these points has been collected, mainly from British Guiana and Trinidad, but at the moment it is rather equivocal. Adamson, Brereton and Johnson emphasise how the large-scale importation of indentured Indians, even when the sugar industry was depressed, reduced employment opportunities for Creoles and forced down their rates of pay [50: 136–9, 165–7, 192–5; 11: 78–87, 105–15; 62: 54–64]. But while wages were cut at times of particular economic difficulty, for example in the later 1840s and the 1880s, according to Moohr and Rodney they could also be increased when conditions improved. The impression given by these authors in their studies of British Guiana up to 1914 is not of a long-term decline of earnings, but rather of a stagnation, at levels still appreciably higher than those found in some other parts of the Caribbean, or in the new plantation areas of Asia [64: 128–37, 146, 163, 212–34; 67: xx, 34–49, 194–8]. Also it is clear that any wage cuts which were achieved fell short of the contemporary decline in the price of sugar (see Graph). Thus the more successful planters must have made technical improvements to raise the productivity of their labour, and for this there is a good deal of independent evidence [50: 167–92; 64: 196–207]. In other words, coercion may have been applied against the labour force, but it was not sufficient by itself to secure the estates' prosperity. Yet without it would wages have been higher, inducing even greater efficiency? The logic of this suggestion is obvious enough; the objection against it is that without substantial political support many planters might not have had enough confidence to innovate in the face of competition from new sources of supply, and the result could have been not a more efficient sugar industry, but one that was seriously weakened, perhaps eliminated altogether, with local incomes suffering as a result. All this raises wider issues about the working of plantation-based economies which must be deferred until the next chapter.

(iv) THE CHARACTER OF SOCIAL RELATIONS

In our discussion of Spanish Caribbean slavery we considered the theory that colonies differed in the character of their social relations and this suggestion has been extended to the period after emancipation. It is argued that the chances of the plantations adapting successfully were reduced if their owners or managers were particularly harsh, and the ex-slaves had strong habits of resistance or independent action. Such attitudes (which were likely to be mutually reinforcing) are believed to have been especially pronounced in Jamaica where, according to Curtin [55], developments were shaped by the conflict between two incompatible cultures, the African and the European. Other islands, however, have been distinguished by their more harmonious atmospheres. Antigua's slaves, according to Burn and Hall [54: 66; 60: 17–25], had by the early nineteenth century assimilated European values to an unusual degree. Partly for this reason it was the only British sugar colony where the planters voluntarily dispensed with apprenticeship, and the ex-slaves were restrained from emigration by their commitment to local churches and friendly societies [60: 40–1]. There is also some evidence that, in their dealings with the freedmen, planters of French origin could be relatively successful. In Trinidad, according to Brereton,

> as slave-owners they had generally established closer, more paternalist relations with their slaves than the English planters, and their influence over the Creole masses in the nineteenth century was certainly stronger .... More French planters were resident than the British, and they tended to own smaller estates, cocoa as well as sugar. [53: 5, 40–1]

Many of Trinidad's free labourers did leave the estates, but Blouet notices that to a greater extent than elsewhere in the 'low-density' colonies of the British West Indies they took up residence on the margins of the already settled area, making themselves available for occasional wage work [51: 445]. Sugar production in Trinidad seems to have been maintained quite well even before the large-scale introduction of indentured labour in the 1850s (see Table III).

In the Spanish islands it may be that racial attitudes were rather less sharply defined than elsewhere, making it easier to draw white and coloured labour into the sugar industry (see above, pp. 28–9). There were also symptoms of 'paternalism' operating to keep ex-slaves attached to the estates, although in Cuba at least many did strike out for themselves. For example, planters often kept stores to supply their workers' needs, perhaps discouraging independent production or marketing and promoting indebtedness [6: *111–12*; 45: *102*; 95: *197–202*]. This was very rare on British West Indian plantations [59: *208–9*], but Bolland has drawn attention to similar arrangements used with considerable effect by employers in the timber-cutting colony of British Honduras [52].

(v) Conclusion

Of the four influences upon the results of emancipation that have been considered it seems that (i) the ratio of population to land area and (iii) political opportunities for the coercion of labour were the most important, at least in the colonies of the northern Europeans. There may have been some scope for emigration from the more densely settled islands, but inertia or uncertainty must have discouraged much of the freed population from moving. Even if restrictive laws could not be thoroughly enforced against the Creoles, it is clear that indentured immigrants were closely controlled. As far as the other two influences are concerned, improved techniques and more generous terms of employment were perhaps of some value in attracting labour, but evidently the ex-slaves' response to monetary inducements was rather weak and, except perhaps in Cuba, where geographical conditions particularly favoured the introduction of centralised milling, mechanisation could not go very far in compensating for a reduced work effort. Finally, as in the period of slavery, it is difficult to show that the character of social relations was an autonomous influence rather than an expression of more fundamental material forces. Thus Curtin considers that the Jamaican planters' ill-considered aggression towards the ex-slaves may have resulted partly from their accumulating economic difficulties [55: *59*]. Trinidad's estates may have been relatively successful in keeping up sugar planting with creole labour because, for technical reasons, it was a less arduous occupation here than in other colonies [44: *202–3*].

It must however be emphasised that, while the estates' fortunes were decisively affected by their ability to command a workforce, whether through the physical scarcity of land for alternative uses or through the exercise of political authority, coercive methods could not by themselves assure the prosperity of a plantation economy. The increase in sugar production on Barbados resulted from refinements in the method of cultivation, although it may have been possible to pursue them only because employers were assured of a reliable local labour supply [20: *116–24*; 58: *258–9*]. On Nevis and Montserrat, where techniques were inferior, quite high densities of population could not prevent the long-term decline of sugar planting (see Table III). Asian immigrants only rescued the estates of British Guiana because efficiency was raised by new processing equipment; Jamaica's planters failed to mechanise and got little benefit from the indenture system. Possibilities for the continuing control of labour and for technical improvement interacted to determine the pattern of adjustment to emancipation.

4 Problems of Economic Development

For the first three-quarters of the nineteenth century the economic history of the Caribbean may be presented in terms of slavery and the effects of its abolition on the sugar industry. Thereafter the themes are more diversified, although sugar remains the most important single influence. In the 1880s its international price was sharply reduced by the growth of subsidised beet sugar exports from continental Europe (see Graph and Table II). Cane sugar could only be kept competitive through the construction of larger and more efficient processing factories, usually supplied by railways from a wider field area than had been customary before. Of the Caribbean producers Cuba, with considerable tracts of flat land, was best suited for these adaptations, and the coastal plains of Puerto Rico also had a significant potential. However in the 1880s and 1890s progress here was inhibited by the uncertainties that followed slave emancipation, and by the political confusion of the last phase of Spanish rule [22: 271–435; 6: 101–7; 94: 65–7]. Many other islands were too small and mountainous to accommodate viable systems of centralised processing and some completely abandoned commercial sugar production in this period. Even the better endowed territories like Trinidad or British Guiana were unable, despite efforts at modernisation, to maintain the growth that they had achieved since the 1850s [79]. There were some compensatory developments: bananas in Jamaica, cocoa in Trinidad and Grenada, gold and rice in British Guiana and Surinam. But there is little doubt that the British, French and Dutch West Indies as a whole suffered economic stagnation from the 1880s to the First World War [86; 41: 13; 15: 161–5].

For Cuba and Puerto Rico, on the other hand, the end of Spanish control in 1898 was a turning point. The United States annexed Puerto Rico as a colony and secured a strong position in Cuba, although allowing it to become formally independent. Both islands were given preferential access to the domestic US sugar market while being at the same time opened up to outside investors, and then the First World War disrupted European beet sugar production to the benefit of cane growers. All this stimulated the rapid growth and modernisation of the Cuban and Puerto Rican sugar industries, increasingly under the control of business interests from the United States [22: *536–56*; 6: *106–17*; 94: *77–8*]. This phase lasted until the early 1920s when competition from European beet sugar revived and caused a sharp fall in prices, later aggravated by the international economic crisis of the 1930s. Cuban sugar suffered particularly because it also lost much of its privileged position in the United States' home market (see Graph and Table II) [78: *157–63*; 91: *86*]. Meanwhile British West Indian sugar production enjoyed a modest revival through the restoration in 1919 of tariff preference in the metropolitan market, for the first time since the mid nineteenth century. Great Britain's experience during the First World War had emphasised the risks of relying upon European beet sugar and demonstrated the merits of relatively secure 'Empire' sources [80: *164–9*]. Also bauxite mining was begun in British Guiana and Surinam, and oil production and refining in Trinidad and the Dutch islands. However these developments were offset by new misfortunes, such as the decline of cocoa growing in consequence of crop disease and competition from West Africa, while the effects of the general depression of the 1930s were widely felt, particularly as it restricted opportunities for migrant labour [11: *177–206*; 23: *141–9*; 75: *75*].

These economic difficulties of the period between the two world wars encouraged popular disturbances, trade union organisation and political nationalism through much of the Caribbean [7: *290–3*; 22: *557–688*]. They also promoted change in public policy. Hitherto it had usually been assumed by those in authority that in so far as economic development was possible within the region, it was best achieved through a more or less unregulated world economy in which the tropics produced raw materials to trade for the manufactured goods of temperate lands. However events after 1914 discredited free trade principles and showed how vulnerable a territory might be if it committed itself almost completely to the export of one or two primary products. Moreover local opinion increasingly disliked the subordinate international status that this implied. So national governments in Cuba and colonial regimes elsewhere attempted to promote social equity and a more balanced economic structure less dominated by sugar. Initially the measures taken may have been trivial and half-hearted, but by the 1940s and 1950s they could have significant effects. The best known instance from this later period was Puerto Rico's 'Operation Bootstrap' which in particular sought to attract outside investment in manufacturing for export to the United States [93]. At the same time Cuba also attempted a programme of diversification away from sugar, although with less striking results [91: 77–81, 144–7]. In the British West Indies the colonial authorities were rather sceptical of the possibilities for industrial development and there was greater emphasis on the modernisation of the sugar industry and peasant agriculture [77: 183–220]. Apart from special government measures, benefits were felt from the flourishing state of the international economy in the 1950s, which opened up new opportunities for mineral exports and emigration, and brought in large numbers of tourists to the Caribbean.

As a result of these various influences, some economic growth has occurred in the region but it has been weak and irregular by the standards of North America or Western Europe. Calculations for Jamaica [14] and British Guiana [64] suggest that output per head of population stagnated in these colonies for a century after slave emancipation. Cuba's per capita income seems to have risen with the rapid development of its sugar industry during the first two decades of the twentieth century but then fell substantially before recovering somewhat; by 1958 income had barely regained the level reached in the early 1920s, although there may have been some long-term improvement in general welfare as a result of redistributive measures [91: 17–19; 88: 72–6; 89: 35–42]. Some territories, most notably Puerto Rico and Jamaica, experienced rapid growth in the 1950s and 1960s (see Table I), but proved ill-adapted to the changed circumstances of the 1970s. So the current position of the Caribbean is usually seen in pessimistic terms, and this has affected work on its economic history, since many authors have been looking into the past for the sources of modern difficulties [76].

For the Caribbean, as for most other parts of the Third World, the problem of economic development has usually been discussed in terms of the region's relationships with what are now the 'advanced' industrial nations of the northern hemisphere. Broadly speaking, two main schools of thought have been in contention. One, sometimes described as 'diffusionist', emphasises the ways in which a 'backward' area can benefit from connections with more de-

48

veloped economies. The export of sugar, for example, makes it possible for a Caribbean island to specialise in the activity for which its soils and climate are best suited, and secure access to capital and entrepreneurial leadership from its trading partners [74: 10–21]. Where such contacts have not brought prosperity, this is attributed by diffusionists to limited natural resources, unfortunate accidents of history, or obstructive details of local culture. Thus it has been suggested that Puerto Rico's continuing poverty in the 1930s, despite the rapid growth of its sugar industry, was partly the result of the pressure of a rapidly growing population on limited areas of cultivable land [97: 61–76, 261]. An analysis of the Cuban economy in the late 1940s by the World Bank emphasised the damage that had been done by arbitrary changes in US trade policy since the 1920s, but also hinted delicately that domestic responses had been weakened by maladministration and habits of political corruption [89: 10–29, 900].

The alternative approach, sometimes called 'dependency theory', denies the diffusionist assumption that economic relations between rich and poor nations should be intrinsically beneficial to both sides, and emphasises how colonial or quasi-colonial status and the associated patterns of trade have limited possibilities for sustained development in the Third World. In its most uncompromising versions, dependency theory claims that the present wealth of the capitalist industrial economies is derived from the Third World's poverty, and vice versa; as it is sometimes put, a 'core' of developed countries has systematically exploited and impoverished a 'periphery'.[5] It is unreasonable and patronising, so the argument runs, to blame local culture as an impediment to the diffusion of 'modern economic growth', particularly in societies like those of the Caribbean that were originally established as appendages to Europe and have remained so thoroughly permeated by external influences. The corrupt politics of pre-revolutionary Cuba, for example, should be seen not as somehow indigenous, but as an expression of the demoralisation resulting from persistent interference by the United States, whose disastrous tariff changes were not anomalous or accidental, but characteristic incidents in the dealings between rich nations and their dependencies [87: 6, 21]. It is even possible to dispute the importance of the apparent natural obstacles to economic development within the Caribbean such as the many small territories and the scarcity of land or other resources. They may have been obviously decisive for small barren islands like Barbuda or St. Eustatius [1: *318, 327*; 60: *59–95*], but the case of the larger units that account for most of the region's inhabitants is less clear. Thus Cuba has significant reserves of both agricultural land and minerals and, as Demas points out [73: *40*], nations of comparable size in Western Europe, such as Holland or Switzerland, have secured considerable economic success. Furthermore it can often be argued, as with the eroded soils of Haiti's peasant holdings [18: *187–231*], or the concentration of British Guiana's population along a narrow coastal strip [24: *280–2*], that the original problem was not deficient natural resources, but the waste and neglect caused by particular social arrangements.

The strongly diffusionist assumptions of nineteenth-century European and North American economic thought first came under serious attack from nationalists in the Caribbean and Latin America during the depressed conditions of the 1920s and 1930s [97]. After the Second World War, however, renewed optimism about prospects for international economic expansion made diffusionism fashionable once more [89; 93; 96], until further difficulties and the radical inspiration of the Cuban Revolution brought another reaction of opinion. Dependency theory was fully articulated and achieved its greatest influence in the 1960s and early 1970s [71; 84; 87; 91; 98]. Subsequently its exponents have been put on the defensive, both by the disappointing practical results of policies which it has inspired, and by detailed academic research [74; 76; 80; 83; 90]. Nevertheless dependency theory still determines much of the agenda for debate on development issues.

(i) EXTERNALLY CONTROLLED ENTERPRISES

A large proportion of the Caribbean's main export activities, particularly the sugar industry, have been under outside ownership and control. From the diffusionist perspective this appears as a useful way of securing improved technology and management [97: *61–76*]. Adherents of dependency theory, on the other hand, often argue that foreign investors have exploited the region by securing excessively high rates of return on their capital. They allege, for example, that in Cuba and Puerto Rico businessmen from the United States were able to take advantage of the confused conditions that followed the overthrow of Spanish rule to secure extensive tracts of sugar land very cheaply [92: *14–74*; 94: *74–6*; 98: *106–9*], and the severe financial crisis that struck Cuba in 1920–1, largely as a result of its close economic ties with the USA, provided an opportunity for more easy acquisitions [87: *16–17*]. Once established, the large new central sugar factories had territorial and credit monopolies which could be used to depress the earnings of local wage labour and cane growers [71: *165–74*; 92: *239–47, 285–6*; 97: *133–46, 274*].

While these arguments may be supported by particular instances, their general strength is uncertain. Thus much of the US control of the Cuban sugar industry was established during the period of speculative excitement in the First World War and its immediate aftermath, probably at inflated prices [87: *14*]. Lebergott suggests that the preference given to Cuban sugar in the US market from 1903 amounted to a free gift from the US taxpayer, most of which went to Cuban landowners and labour [90]. No consensus has been reached on the profitability of externally controlled enterprises. Some authors consider it to have been relatively high [9: *436–7*; 91: *67*; 88: *425–6*], while others emphasise how from the 1930s rates of return were constrained by economic depression, the growing strength of trade unions, and nationalist legislation in favour of cane growers [97; 80: *319–64*]. However Zanetti and García argue in the case of the United Fruit Company's Cuban sugar operations that the modest reported profits were the result of exaggerated depreciation allowances [92: *176–80, 439*].

Another possibility is that the Caribbean has suffered from the common tendency for foreign firms to integrate their local activities with secondary processing elsewhere, for example the production of raw sugar in Cuba or Trinidad combined with its refining in the USA or Great Britain [71: *114–53*]. Such arrangements might be exploitative because there has sometimes been a very considerable degree of monopoly at the secondary stage which could perhaps be used against Caribbean producers: the 'Sugar Trust' dominated cane sugar refining in the USA during the first decade of the twentieth century, and Tate and Lyle has done so in Great Britain since the 1920s [78: *204*; 87: *5*; 80: *135–42*]. Also it has been suggested that firms with heavy commitments of fixed capital to metropolitan processing plants might prefer to maximise their production by keeping down the cost of inputs, even though the Caribbean could sometimes be better served by restricted output and higher prices.

This was said to have been a point of contention between US and national sugar interests in Cuba during the 1920s [87: *29–31*]. Furthermore, with vertical integration there was scope for 'transfer pricing', the manipulation of intra-firm prices to artificially depress the proportion of profits accruing within the Caribbean, in order to minimise liability to local taxation [71: *133*; 92: *175*]. However, each of these points is debatable. According to Lebergott the market power of the Sugar Trust was quite limited [90: *235–6*]; quota restrictions were eventually imposed on Cuban sugar producers, although Benjamin argues that this was with the consent of the US firms [87: *31*]; Chalmin's detailed study seems to exonerate Tate and Lyle from the charge of transfer pricing [80: *405, 647*]. Perhaps our provisional judgement should be that in the early decades of the twentieth century outside investors often did have unusual economic power, although as time passed some countervailing influences developed. But we have no clear sense of the effect that all this had upon local incomes.

(ii) THE TERMS OF TRADE AND THEORIES OF 'UNEQUAL EXCHANGE'

Whatever the results of the structure of individual enterprises, it can also be argued that the Caribbean, like many other parts of the world, has suffered from a secular deterioration in the terms of trade between the exporters of primary products and the industrial nations. According to this theory in its original form, there has been a persistent tendency for the price of raw materials to fall relatively to manufactured goods, because the former are, for example, subject to lower income elasticities of demand, or liable to displacement by synthetic substitutes. Yet there is much uncertainty, fully reflected in the literature on the Caribbean, whether the terms of trade have moved in this way [72: *273, 293*; 89: *751*; 97: *37–40*; 84: *200–2*]. There are also other difficulties. So far we have considered movements in the *commodity* or *net barter* terms of trade, but W. A. Lewis has developed an argument which emphasises instead the *factoral* terms of trade, that is the value of a factor's production in terms of imports.[6] In his view the price of labour used in the growing of tropical export crops, and thus the price of these crops in international trade, has usually been depressed by its low productivity in local food growing, which is the main alternative activity. Conversely, in the developed countries agricultural labour has become more efficient, and thus industrial wages and industrial output prices have been sustained at relatively high levels. For example, a German engineering worker enjoys a higher income than an Indian tea picker partly because a German farmer growing wheat is more productive than an Indian farmer growing rice or millet. However, whatever the general merits of this theory, the extent to which it can be applied to the Caribbean is unclear, for while the average productivity of labour in local subsistence farming has undoubtedly been low (see below, pp. 56–60), over much of the region the size of the subsistence sector relative to export activities has often been rather small, so its influence on returns to labour is doubtful. It is true that through the system of indentured labour the Caribbean was for a time linked with great reservoirs of low-productivity agriculture in India and China, but there is room for disagreement about the effects that this had upon labour markets (see above, pp. 40–2).

(iii) Obstacles to technical change in Caribbean sugar production

Another suggestion, one which we have encountered already (see above, p. 41), is that technical progress in the Caribbean was retarded by employers' preference for 'cheap labour' rather than increases in productivity as a means of securing their profits. This is said to have been a habit established under slavery, and perpetuated after emancipation, especially through the indenture system [76: 37–51]. But there are difficulties with this argument both on points of detail – how cheap was Caribbean labour by international standards and to what extent had sugar planters as a class eschewed innovation? (see above, pp. 20–8, 38) – and also on its broader assumption that technical change was determined by the state of local labour markets. For a crop such as tea, grown exclusively in poor tropical countries, it may be reasonable to suppose that the low opportunity cost of labour was the main reason why employers did not trouble themselves to invent more productive methods. But a feature distinguishing sugar from other tropical crops is that it has been grown in developed countries also, relying upon improved techniques as well as tariff protection to accommodate relatively high and rising wage costs. In the nineteenth century processing was the main area of innovation; more recently plant breeding and

53

field mechanisation have been equally significant [78: *125–54*]. In principle such developments should have been usually available for Caribbean producers to imitate. Yet they have often been slow to do so, and it is not always clear that this is adequately explained by 'cheap labour', which sometimes may have been as much a consequence as a cause of technical retardation.

One problem was an unfavourable topography, as with the failure in some of the smaller islands to centralise processing [79: *83*; 74: *15*], although the main producers had substantial areas of level land quite suitable for innovation. In the longer settled colonies, such as Barbados, family pride of ownership and accumulated complications of title may have inhibited the consolidation of properties into larger and more efficient units [79: *34–5, 126–7*], but generally estates seem to have changed hands quite easily [6: *106–17*; 19: *70–1*; 80: *313–14*]. Probably a much more serious source of difficulty has been the Caribbean's marginal position in externally controlled trading systems, leaving it unusually vulnerable to sudden changes in fortune, reflected by the wide fluctuations which have occurred in sugar's international price (see Graph). The British West Indies were severely affected by the loss of tariff protection in their British market in the late 1840s, and again by the appearance of subsidised beet sugar exports from continental Europe in the 1880s. 'Free trade' ideology and metropolitan interests that benefited from cheap sugar, such as the confectionery industry, obstructed any effective action against these subsidies until the Brussels Convention of 1902 [9: *374–91*; 50: *214–32*]. Again, Cuba's sugar industry, hitherto highly progressive, suffered severely in its trade relations with the USA during the 1920s and 1930s (see above, p. 47), and in reaction a very restrictive system of regulations and quotas was developed which prevented much further technical improvement [78: *83–5*; 91: *59–69*]. It is noticeable that the most innovative cane sugar growing areas elsewhere in the world – for example, Hawaii, Louisiana and Queensland – have usually had access to protected markets [78: *151*].

The damage done to the Caribbean by market instability is obvious enough, but the preferential trading arrangements made available by the colonial powers during the course of this century, such as the British Commonwealth Sugar Agreement begun in 1951 [82: *146–9*], have reduced this problem to a certain extent. Yet Hagelberg argues that the region has not taken full advantage of the

54

opportunities thus offered: export quotas have not been met, even at prices substantially above those of the 'free' world market [74]. One immediate cause of this failure seems to have been the slow progress, by international standards, of field mechanisation, at least partly because of the hostility of the local labour force expressed by increasingly powerful trade unions and widely supported by local opinion. In Jamaica, for example, the import of cane-cutting machines was officially prohibited until 1969 [80: *337–40, 495*]. Of course, labour opposition to labour-saving technical change is common in capitalist societies, but it seems to have been unusually obstructive in the Caribbean. How should this be explained? Was it mainly a defensive response to the experience of adversity, as suggested for Cuba from the 1930s [89: *357–9*]? On the other hand, Jamaica after the Second World War experienced a period of economic growth, including substantial increases in real wages for its sugar workers, and yet the failure to secure sufficient compensating increases in productivity impaired the international competitiveness of its sugar industry [74: *136*; 84: *91–100*]. These difficulties, even in conditions of rising prosperity, may still have largely resulted from the continuing and justified fear of unemployment. However another possible influence is the marked mistrust between employers and employed, an effect of the rigid social stratification traditional in plantation agriculture and its associations with slavery, indentured labour and foreign ownership. Whatever degree of 'exploitation' may have been originally involved in these relationships, there is no doubt that they have been fruitful sources of popular resentment, especially in the twentieth century as nationalist and egalitarian feelings have spread [21: *279–81, 312*; 96: *59–61*; 77: *236–40*].

At the moment we have no clear idea of the importance of these various influences, and perhaps the most promising line of inquiry will be through a comparative approach both within and outside the region. Thus Chalmin suggests that Tate and Lyle found it easier during the 1950s and 1960s to innovate on its estates in Trinidad than in Jamaica[80: *316–65*]. To what extent was this the result of a generally more favourable economic context in Trinidad which mitigated the problem of redeploying displaced labour, always a serious consideration in such small and highly specialised territories? How significant were the relatively harmonious social relations which have been attributed to this island since the nineteenth century ([68: 4–10], and see above, p. 43)? Looking outside the Caribbean, there are several possible explanations for the unusually high productivity of Hawaii's sugar industry: superior natural resources, a helpful social climate (perhaps because of freedom from a legacy of slavery), preferential access to the US market and the cushion against unemployment offered by heavy military and naval expenditures from the 1930s [78: 132–60]. There is also, in Deerr's words, stressing the contrast between Hawaii and the Caribbean, 'the absence of absentee proprietors, with their place taken by resident owners of virile Nordic extraction' [2: I, 258].

(iv) PEASANTRIES AND FOOD GROWING

Apart from technical retardation in its principal export sector, the Caribbean's other most obvious economic weakness has been in the inadequate development of alternative activities. We shall consider first the problems of food production for local consumption. Many islands have come to rely heavily upon food imports, to the detriment of their balance of payments and thus of their potential for economic growth [73: 104–5; 84: 120–1], despite government efforts to promote agricultural diversification, usually through small-scale peasant farming. For much of the nineteenth century, official thinking almost exclusively favoured the sugar estates, but eventually this bias was softened as they proved incapable of ensuring a reasonable prosperity. The first results of this change in emphasis were 'settlement schemes' making land available to culti-vators in small lots, experimentally in a few colonies from the 1860s, and more generally from the 1890s [14: 218; 85: 261–3; 98: 145–6; 77: 193–4]. Governments have also come to sponsor technic-al advisory services, cooperatives, credit institutions, marketing boards and general rural amenities, such as roads, schools and water supplies but, despite these efforts, the efficiency of small-scale agriculture has in general remained very low [10: 95–127; 84: 84–91; 18].

One explanation is that such measures have frequently been weak and ineffectual. Elite self-interest and force of habit ensured that resources were still disproportionately concentrated upon the plantations, while settlement schemes were often little more than palliatives for social discontent, introduced at times of depression and using inferior land [71: 24; 77: 193–9]. In any case, administrators in a region so strongly influenced by the culture and technical assumptions of the USA or western Europe had little expertise that could usefully be applied to small-scale tropical farming. Thus during the 1950s efforts to improve rice production in British Guiana and Cuba relied too much upon mechanisation [89: *853*; 82: *89–122*]; this contrasted with Japan's earlier success as a colonial power in propagating her techniques of intensive rice growing in Korea and Taiwan. Also the scarcity of land relative to population within the region was very discouraging; even the British could have some success in promoting peasant development where natural resources were more favourable, as in parts of Africa. But when due account has been taken of these points, the impression still remains that in the Caribbean the rate of return to any given level of government effort or expenditure on behalf of peasant agriculture has been remarkably low, and the scarcity of land cannot be the only reason, for much of it has been incompletely used [1: *346*; 4: *296–301*]. Therefore many authors have emphasised also the poor morale of rural populations, expressed in mutual mistrust, an incapacity for communal action, and a weak commitment to agriculture as a full-time activity, especially among the medium-scale farmers who elsewhere have often been important sources of local leadership and progress [21: *152–60, 225–6*; 77: *70–6*; 18: *595–8*]. Improved schools, for example, have frequently served not as a means of producing more intelligent farmers (a common hope of governments), but as a route to other occupations [21: *259*]. There is wide agreement that such attitudes result from the long ascendancy of the plantations, but uncertainty about the exact historical processes which brought this about.

In examining the problem, studies of British Guiana by Adamson and Mandle [19; 50] imply that if after emancipation the plantations had not been artificially supported by the colonial government at the expense of the emerging population of small-holders, then a prosperous, diversified economy would have developed. The argument assumes, first, that the former slaves had a high level of economic aspirations and skills as an enthusiastic 'proto-peasantry', second, that the estates kept a substantial capacity for coercion with which to frustrate this potential, and third, that it was the ensuing disappointments which gave peasant farming its poor reputation, so that subsequent efforts at reform could achieve little. However, there are possibilities for disagreement on the first two of these assumptions (see above, pp. 38–42). It can be argued that the coercive power of the estates was limited, implying perhaps that the mediocre performance of small-scale agriculture was a consequence either of unfavourable natural resources, or the incapacity of the ex-slaves themselves which resulted from the degradations of slavery and the attitudes that it had fostered. Thus in areas such as the British Windward Islands where after emancipation plantations were relatively weak, at least in terms of their control of land, creole peasantries did not become especially prosperous [85: 259–60]. To take the most extreme case, in Haiti the estates were virtually eliminated by the 1840s [17: 74–9], and yet the island has become the poorest in the Caribbean. But landownership may not be the most satisfactory measure of the estates' influence. Many of Haiti's difficulties have clearly come from the selfish and incompetent rule of its mainly mulatto elite, a product of the eighteenth-century plantations [17; 100: 255–407]. In this way the plantations could still inhibit development long after their physical disappearance. Elsewhere freedmen may have got sufficient access to land to gain a measure of independence from the surviving plantations, but only on very insecure terms, as squatters or tenants, which restricted them to the most rudimentary shifting agriculture.

The plantations might also weaken peasantries without being systematically coercive. By offering paid employment they fostered a preference for imported wheat flour, rice, beans and salt fish, at the expense of locally grown food [10: 155–7; 21: 200, 226, 312]. Their example led peasants towards specialisation in export crops, such as bananas, cocoa or coffee, which limited the development of agricultural skills and were vulnerable to market changes or plant diseases [85: 257]. Much of the employment offered by the sugar estates was confined to a few months of intensive but relatively well-paid effort during the harvest, encouraging habits of migrant labour and a reluctance to look upon a small holding as an intensive occupation [21: 163; 97: 218]. This particularly depressed yields of vegetable crops, many of which, unlike sugar cane, require continuous attention. Jefferson and Beckford argue that by their competition planters prevented smaller farmers from recruiting supplementary wage labour [71: 26; 84: 87], and in Cuba it is said that from the 1940s the fixing by law of agricultural wages at the rates payable in sugar inhibited employment in the rather less remunerative food crops, even on estate land [89: 96]. Finally, in so

58

far as peasants depended upon the prosperity of the plantation sector for their markets, they shared its vicissitudes. For instance, in Jamaica they were damaged by the crisis of the sugar estates that followed the elimination of preferential British import duties after 1846 [58: *307–16*; 59: *170, 196*].

Because of this variety of possible influences it is difficult to establish how far the problems of creole peasantries have been the result of intrinsic weaknesses, possible results of slavery, and how far of the external constraints imposed by the continuing influence of the estates. The problem may be approached through comparison with other groups that had never been slaves. For example, some observers consider the descendants of Indian indentured labourers to have been more committed farmers, with a greater capacity for accumulation and innovation in a rural context, shown by their development of rice production in Trinidad, British Guiana and Surinam, while the local Creoles have preferred migration to the towns, mines, oilfields or forest industries [23: *235–46*; 75: *157–8*]. One East Indian advantage in agriculture often mentioned is a more cohesive family structure, less disrupted than that of the Creoles during the period of coerced labour, and less likely to produce the fragmentation and indeterminate claims that have become characteristic of much creole landholding [81].

However, these differences between East Indians and Creoles can be explained in other ways. By the time that the Indians came to be released from their indentures in large numbers, official opinion had begun to see virtue in small-scale farming, and there was a practical need to dissuade them from claiming their rights to repatriation. So they received early government assistance in establishing themselves on the land which had usually been denied to the freed slaves [68: *274–7*; 50: *94–8*]. It is true that in Surinam government policy immediately after emancipation was relatively generous, but here, according to Van Lier, much of the creole peasantry was severely damaged by the disease that destroyed its cocoa trees. When allowance is made for this early misfortune he doubts whether the Creoles have shown any special inaptitude for agriculture [23: *223–46*]. And there are difficulties in evaluating the undoubted modern weakness of the creole nuclear family. Recent research by Higman suggests that under slavery family life may have been more structured than was once supposed, so perhaps subsequent instability was as much a consequence as a cause of economic adversity [35:

156–73; 24: *200–3*]. For example, the pressures on both men and women to travel seeking wage work encouraged irregular unions. In Jamaica Edith Clarke found quite strong family ties and community institutions in an unusually prosperous mixed farming district, but severe disorganisation among migrant cane cutters [81]. In any case, although in the Caribbean East Indians may on the whole have been better farmers than the Creoles, by international standards their performance is still rather poor [15: *76–9*]. Also many of the weaknesses attributed to creole peasantries can be found among the mainly white population of the Puerto Rican interior [21; 95]. It seems, then, that the Caribbean's general circumstances, or the position of the plantations in particular, have been more influential than any specific 'legacy of slavery' [24: *280–92*].

There may be wide agreement that sugar planting has been unhelpful, in one way or another, to the progress of peasant farming, but it need not follow that the plantations have retarded the general economic development of the Caribbean, although this deduction is frequently made [50: *255–66*; 71; 76]. Sugar, even when produced rather inefficiently, has remained an unusually high-yielding crop. In Puerto Rico during the 1940s, for example, an acre of land under cane gave the same revenue as four acres of sweet potatoes, or twelve and a half acres of corn [74: *16*]. Dependency theory, while recognising such differences, has sought to account for them in terms of the more fertile land controlled by the estates, the long-standing bias in investment and research towards the export staple, or subsidies on metropolitan food supplies [71: *28, 178–9, 226*]. However, points of this kind have not been supported with much factual detail, so there is still a good deal of force in the diffusionists' argument that sugar cane, with its high output and labour requirements per acre, and its capacity to survive drought or hurricane and to prevent soil erosion, was particularly suitable for the densely populated territories of the Caribbean [74: *10–16*; 97: *295–6*]. For much of the region comparative advantage in sugar may have been so pronounced that it outweighed the damaging incidental effects of plantation agriculture.

(v) MANUFACTURING

Finally, the region has had only limited success in establishing manufacturing industry, despite the inducements offered under many modern development plans [91: *135–55*; 84: *125–47*]. One constraint has been the problems of agriculture already discussed, which impaired local purchasing power. Yet this cannot provide a complete explanation, for elsewhere, notably in East Asia, it has proved possible for small, densely populated territories, some of them originally with lower per capita incomes than the main Caribbean islands, to develop manufacturing, largely on the basis of exports. Certainly Puerto Rico secured substantial economic growth in this way during the 1950s and 1960s, but her achievement has not been sustained or successfully imitated within the region, and seems to have been the result mainly of privileged access to the US market [93].

Once again, much emphasis has been placed on the Caribbean's unusually dependent position within the international economy and the pernicious influence of the plantations. Over most of our period the colonial powers, regarding their possessions as sources of raw materials and outlets for manufactures, deliberately inhibited the development of local processing, sugar refining for example, by formal restrictions or tax measures [78: *162–3*; 72: *13–35*]. Although from the 1920s they became rather more sympathetic towards economic diversification, permission was still withheld from the 'artificial' inducements, such as tariff protection, that were coming into use in India and Latin America by this time. Even Cuba, nominally an independent state, found its ability to tax the import of manufactured goods severely limited by the need to keep access to the US market for its sugar [91: *141–5*; 88: *35, 61*; 87: *38–40, 178–84*]. The traditional reliance upon staple exports is said to have fostered a taste for imported manufactures at the expense of local production, just as with foodstuffs[84: *137*], and perhaps also inhibited capital accumulation. It is alleged, first, that business profits, often an important source of savings, have accrued mainly to externally controlled enterprises for remittance elsewhere [94: *86*], second, that through their close contact with much richer metropolitan societies Caribbean populations have come to aspire to high standards of consumption, at the expense of personal savings [73: *114–18*; 98: *228–9*], and third, that the structure of financial institutions has prevented local capital from being used in support of new activities [82: *271–3*]. Some writers, however, consider the weakness of local entrepreneurship to have been a much more fundamental difficulty [14: *xxi–xxii*]. Even when de-

61

liberate measures were taken by governments to favour industrial development, very often it was outsiders who responded most vigorously [87: *39*; 89: *735*; 96: *50*]. One possible reason for this is the long ascendancy of outside interests in the plantation export sector, because of its heavy financial and technical requirements, or political discrimination by colonial regimes [21: *191*; 87: *10–17*; 95]. With chances of business leadership pre-empted, the local middle class was directed towards government service and professions such as teaching, medicine and the law [75: *305–6*; 98: *106–10*].

The Caribbean's location within the international economy is also said to have had unfortunate effects on the working of labour markets, although the details of this point are disputed. During the course of the twentieth century unemployment has become conspicuous in many territories, and manufacturing has shown little capacity to absorb it, even when output has grown quite rapidly [73: *107–12*; 84: *28–32*]. Dependency theory argues that this is an inevitable result of modern 'industrialisation by invitation' policies, which in default of local initiative have relied heavily upon attracting investors from Europe or North America, bringing with them the labour-saving techniques appropriate to high-wage economies, and building plants that have few local linkages [98: *226*; 84: *145–7*]. Diffusionists, on the other hand, stress the restrictive effects on employment arising from the high wages of Caribbean labour in relation to its productivity [83]. In Cuba before 1959 and in the British West Indies much of this problem of cost efficiency has been attributed to the growing militancy of trade unions, itself perhaps largely a consequence of the sugar industry's unfortunate history [22: *1172–9*; 77: *224–42*]. In Puerto Rico minimum wage legislation resulting from the island's close association with the United States has been suggested as a cause of unemployment [99: *302–6*].

Obviously sugar planting has put special difficulties in the way of industrial development, but it would be unfair to give a wholly negative impression. If the Caribbean had a comparative advantage in sugar production, then commitment to it could be expected to raise incomes and the demand for manufactured goods. It is true that a large proportion of any demand generated in this way would be met from external sources, as dependency theorists emphasise [71: *186–7*], but they have not been able to show that an increase in the relative importance of plantation exports usually reduced expenditure on local manufactures. The calculations of Eisner and

Moohr imply that on the eve of the First World War industrial production per head of population was higher in British Guiana, where sugar planting had been maintained, than in Jamaica, where it had been severely curtailed since emancipation [14: 88; 64]. Nearly all of the elaborate machinery required for sugar processing was imported, but maintenance work gave rise to significant engineering and iron-founding establishments in both Cuba and Puerto Rico [16: 377; 96: 64]. Foreign investors did not completely exclude native entrepreneurs. Even in Cuba, where US interests were so powerful, nationals increased the share of sugar production which they milled from 22 per cent in 1940 to 62 per cent in 1958, and the Cuban Julio Lobo became reputedly the world's most powerful sugar trader [88: 68–9; 80: 274–6]. Apart from primary exports, substantial opportunities remained in general commerce, a sector which in other regions has proved a useful nursery for manufacturers [96: 32–65]. The apparent weakness of innovative or competitive spirit among Caribbean businessmen may have been due mainly to the constraints of limited island markets, whose small size was a standing invitation to collusive and monopolistic practices [84: 127–8; 89: 12, 57–65, 187–90; 91: 149–53]. Sugar plantations have been criticised for supporting large numbers of poorly motivated field labourers [21: 163–7; 71: 204–8], but they also required a considerable skilled cadre [89: 71]. The factories established in Puerto Rico during the 1950s drew workers from the estate proletariat rather than from the peasantry of the interior, and observers were on the whole favourably impressed by the quality of the recruits [99: 296–9]. Although in many ways plantation agriculture has been unhelpful to the growth of manufacturing, it cannot be assumed that the Caribbean had the option of some other economic system which would have offered a better basis for industrialisation.

(vi) CONCLUSION

Dependency theory provides a forceful and stimulating interpretation of recent Caribbean economic history, but it has proved vulnerable to criticism on points of detail. As we saw in the discussion of externally controlled enterprises and theories of 'unequal exchange', there are doubts whether plantations have secured unreasonably high rates of profit for metropolitan capital, or imposed a long-term deterioration in the terms of trade upon the territories where they are located. On the other hand, it is quite clear that the rate of growth of efficiency in Caribbean sugar production has been low, by the standards of the developed world, and that many aspects of a plantation economy tend to obstruct the development of peasant farming and manufacturing industry. Yet while dependency theory has succeeded in accumulating instances and arguments on these points, it has conspicuously failed to get to grips with the fundamental issue of comparative advantage. Diffusionists can still argue that sugar, for all its faults, offered the best and most intensive use of the Caribbean's limited natural resources. Exponents of the concept of dependency have not been precise enough in the weighing of costs and benefits convincingly to refute this part of the diffusionist case. Adamson, for example, during the course of an unusually thorough critique of sugar planting in British Guiana, passes over in a few lines the problem of whether any other activity could have sustained the elaborate system of sea defences and drainage that was required for settlement on this colony's coastal lowlands [50: 262].

The application of dependency theory to the Caribbean often involves questionable argument by analogy or hypothesis, implying that at various stages in the history of the region there was some alternative path open to it, more self-sufficient and ultimately more rewarding than the way that was actually taken: in the seventeenth century, colonisation with small-scale, family-operated farms, as in parts of North America, rather than with slaves and plantations; after emancipation, a prosperous creole peasantry rather than artificially supported sugar estates [19: 60–8; 71: 44–7]; in 1898, real independence instead of United States hegemony for Cuba and Puerto Rico, perhaps with tobacco and coffee (potentially the crops of small farmers), instead of sugar as the main export staples [4: 145–62]. According to this line of argument, family farms offered scope for individual initiative, while plantations entailed subordination and restricted opportunities for the mass of the population. Societies based upon family farms have been racially homogeneous, securing egalitarian ideologies, internal stability and political independence, while plantation societies have been racially diverse, highly stratified and politically insecure [21: 330; 71: 35–6, 192].

Yet what were the practical possibilities for the development of a prosperous yeoman agriculture in the Caribbean during our period? It is fanciful to expect that the growing of yams or plantains on a tropical island would offer the same scope for the development of economic skills and the accumulation of capital as, for example, wheat farming in North America. The latter brought local processing requirements and opportunities for long-distance marketing which the former lacked almost completely. The fortunes of Caribbean tobacco and coffee growers in the twentieth century have been quite undistinguished, and arguments attributing their difficulties almost entirely to the influence of the United States have not carried conviction [21: *108–98*; 87: *8–9*; 94: *81–5*]. Up to 1950, when the Caribbean's leading economic activity was still sugar planting, the territories which were most heavily involved in it had as a rule made the most progress; for example, despite their many difficulties, the measured per capita income of both Cuba and Puerto Rico was greater than that of the Dominican Republic (see Table I). On balance it seems likely that the Caribbean has gained more than it has lost by participation in the international economy, even through plantation agriculture, although the margin of advantage may have been narrower than for some other parts of the world.

5 General Conclusion

This survey has considered the economic history of the Caribbean under three headings: slavery, adjustments to emancipation, and problems of economic development. On each subject there has been progress, although unresolved problems still remain. Caribbean plantation slavery, it seems, had a greater adaptability than was once supposed; nevertheless external pressures undoubtedly weighed heavily upon it in the early nineteenth century, and more research will be needed, especially at the level of the individual property and for the Spanish islands, to clarify the planters' position. The estates' adjustments to emancipation were determined by a mixture of coercion and technical innovation, but the interaction between these two elements has not yet been completely understood. Over the longer term, the continuation of sugar planting was probably helpful to general economic development, but this judgement depends upon a complicated balance of costs and benefits.

Apart from the problems which are specific to one or other of the three topics, there is a more general difficulty in drawing together any conclusions into a sustained and coherent narrative, because of the ways in which primary research has been compartmentalised. Originally at least, historians considered Caribbean slavery mainly as an issue in metropolitan politics (see above, pp. 18–19). Also slavery has exercised a lurid fascination as a particularly brutal social regime, reflected in the enthusiasm for work on slave demography and rebellion (see above, pp. 23–5). These preoccupations, however useful, have to some extent diverted attention from slavery's characteristics as, among other things, a system of production. Hence there is continuing uncertainty on such issues as profitability, technology and investment (see above, pp. 20–3). As for the sequel to emancipation, some of the most distinguished treatments have approached it very largely as a problem of imperial administration, with plantation economics treated as a conditioning influence rather than a central concern [54; 55; 58]. One result has been a heavy reliance for this period upon contemporary published accounts, the reports of colonial officials, or parliamentary inquiries. This material was often generated by the controversies of the time, for example over the need for immigration schemes, and cannot be accepted as wholly reliable testimony on the ex-slaves' work attitudes, or the condition of the estates. Very few investigations have gone further, by studying the records kept by sugar plantations as they tried to adapt to the new order and relating their experiences comprehensively to the pre-emancipation background [30: 281–313]. Finally, most discussion of long-term economic development has remained in the hands of writers concerned above all with current events and policies, who tend to smooth over the complexities of evidence from a remoter past [71]. Thus Mandle's recent study assumes that the economic difficulties of the modern Caribbean can be traced back to a plantation agriculture in which, both before and after emancipation, the coercive aspect was so marked as almost completely to stifle any possibilities for technical progress [76: 37–52]. He takes no account of work by Bennett, Green, and others [28; 57; 59], which might qualify this opinion.

Recent work on American slavery suggests caution in evaluating slavery in the Caribbean. North American plantation slavery used to be seen as chronically inefficient, yet there is now evidence that the southern slave states were quite productive, their backwardness relative to the rest of the USA only becoming pronounced after emancipation [46: 247–57; 70: 51–3]. Clearly part of the post-emancipation decline occurred simply because the ex-slaves chose to take advantage of their freedom by working less hard, and to this extent the situation of the southern United States in the later nineteenth century can be interpreted as a result of the attitudes established under slavery. But other influences may also have been important, such as the destruction caused by the Civil War, or a decline in the rate of growth in demand for cotton [56: 206–20; 70: 86–97]. While debate on the relative importance of these factors has so far been inconclusive, at least a reasoned attempt is being made to distinguish the heritage of slavery from other forces. This task has not yet been undertaken for the Caribbean, even though here too (in the British West Indies at least) there may have been a pattern of fairly high productivity under slavery with severe retardation only after emancipation [70: 53–5]. There is also a similar range of alternative causes in need of consideration, such as the problems of markets and unfavourable natural resources. One reason why the discussion of long-term development has been carried further for the southern United States is that it builds upon fuller research into the original slave economy, carried out in a more analytical way, and with an eye to wider issues. Similar work is required for the Caribbean.

Notes

1. Currency conversions have been made at official exchange rates. Purchasing power parities would be more appropriate but are not available for a sufficient number of Caribbean territories. Because of this and other problems of estimation, the figures given can only be very approximate, especially as a measure of welfare. See A. Maddison, 'A Comparison of Levels of GDP Per Capita in Developed and Developing Countries, 1700–1980', *Journal of Economic History*, XLIII (1983); [76: *26–36*].

2. This study will include British Honduras (now Belize), British Guiana (now Guyana), French Guiana, and the Dutch colony of Surinam, all lying on the American continent but so isolated from their hinterlands as to be islands in effect.

3. The term 'Creole' has a variety of usages [75: *32–3*]. In this study it refers to persons of African ancestry born within the Caribbean.

4. Haiti's slave rebellion began in 1791 and had been completed by the end of the decade. Attempts were made to maintain various kinds of forced labour until the 1820s [17]. Elsewhere the dates for the final abolition of slavery, with any subsequent period of regulated labour, are: Dominican Republic, 1820s; British colonies, 1834–8; French colonies, 1848; Danish colonies, 1849–61; Dutch colonies, 1848, 1863–73; Puerto Rico, 1873–6; Cuba, 1880–6.

5. A. G. Frank, *Capitalism and Underdevelopment in Latin America* (New York, 1967); I. Wallerstein, *The Capitalist World-Economy* (Cambridge, 1979). For critical evaluations of dependency theory, see J. Forbes Munro, *Britain in Tropical Africa 1880–1960* (1984); Bill Albert, *South America and the World Economy from Independence to 1930* (1983).

6. W. A. Lewis, *Growth and Fluctuations 1870–1913* (1978), pp. 188–93.

Select Bibliography

Unless otherwise stated the place of publication of books is London.

REFERENCE

L. Comitas, *The Complete Caribbeana, 1900–1975*, 4 vols (New York, 1977) is the standard bibliography.

Information about current publications is given in:

The Handbook of Latin American Studies (currently Austin, Texas), yearly from 1936.
British Bulletin of Publications on Latin America, The Caribbean, Portugal and Spain, twice yearly from 1949.

Most of the books listed below have comprehensive bibliographies.

GENERAL STUDIES

[1] H. Blume, *The Caribbean Islands* (1974). Mainly geographical, with some history.
[2] N. Deerr, *The History of Sugar*, 2 vols (1949–50). A worldwide survey.
[3] E. Goveia, *A Study on the Historiography of the British West Indies to the End of the Nineteenth Century* (Mexico City, 1956).
[4] M. M. Horowitz (ed.), *Peoples and Cultures of the Caribbean* (New York, 1971).
[5] F. W. Knight, *The Caribbean: Genesis of a Fragmented Nationalism* (New York, 1978).
[6] S. Mintz, *Caribbean Transformations* (Chicago, 1974). A

collection of some of this author's particularly influential essays.

[7]   J. H. Parry and P. Sherlock, *A Short History of the West Indies*, 3rd edn (1981).

[8]   E. Williams, *British Historians and the West Indies* (Port of Spain, 1964).

[9]   ——, *From Columbus to Castro* (1970).

STUDIES OF INDIVIDUAL TERRITORIES

[10] N. Ashcraft, *Colonialism and Underdevelopment: Processes of Political Economic Change in British Honduras* (New York, 1973).

[11] B. Brereton, *A History of Modern Trinidad 1783–1962* (1981).

[12] A. Buffon, *Monnaie et Crédit en Économie Coloniale. Contribution à l'Histoire Économique de la Guadeloupe, 1635–1919* (Basse-Terre, Guadeloupe, 1979).

[13] C. Degn, *Die Schimmelmanns im atlantischen Dreieckshandel: Gewinn und Gewissen* (Neumünster, 1974). Includes an account of one of the main absentee-owned sugar estates on St. Croix when this island was a Danish colony.

[14] G. Eisner, *Jamaica 1830–1930: A Study in Economic Growth* (Manchester, 1961). Uses national income accounting techniques.

[15] C.C. Goslinga, *A Short History of the Netherlands Antilles and Surinam* (The Hague, 1979).

[16] J. Le Riverend Brusone, *Historia Económica de Cuba*, 4th edn (Havana, 1974).

[17] J. G. Leyburn, *The Haitian People*, 2nd edn (New Haven, 1966). Historical background since the eighteenth century.

[18] M. Lundahl, *Peasants and Poverty: A Study of Haiti* (1979). Similar in scope to [17], but with more thorough economic analysis.

[19] J. R. Mandle, *The Plantation Economy: Population and Economic change in Guyana 1838–1960* (Philadelphia, 1973). See also [50].

[20] O. P. Starkey, *The Economic Geography of Barbados* (New York, 1939). Mainly history since the seventeenth century.

[21] J. Steward *et al.*, *The People of Puerto Rico* (Urbana, 1956). The results of a survey made in the late 1940s by a team of

social anthropologists with an unusual sensitivity to recent historical change.

[22] H. Thomas, *Cuba: The Pursuit of Freedom* (New York, 1971). A general history of the island, including much economic information.

[23] R. A. J. Van Lier, *Frontier Society: A Social Analysis of the History of Surinam*, 2nd edn (The Hague, 1971).

THE LAST YEARS OF SLAVERY

(See also [13]–[16]; [20]–[23]; [50]; [54]; [57]; [58])

(i) General

[24] M. Craton (ed.), *Roots and Branches: Current Directions in Slave Studies* (Toronto, 1979). Like [25], the proceedings of a recent conference.

[25] V. Rubin and A. Tuden (eds), *Comparative Perspectives on Slavery in New World Plantation Societies* (New York, 1976).

(ii) British West Indies

[26] R. T. Anstey, 'Capitalism and Slavery: a Critique', *Economic History Review*, 2nd Series, XXI (1968). Takes issue with [40].

[27] R. K. Aufhauser, 'The Profitability of Slavery in the British Caribbean', *Journal of Interdisciplinary History*, V (1974). Argues against [37] that plantations remained profitable up to emancipation. See also [39].

[28] J. H. Bennett, *Bondsmen and Bishops* (Berkeley, 1958). A study of some Barbados plantations, emphasising improvements in the slaves' material condition.

[29] S. G. Checkland, *The Gladstones: A Family Biography 1764–1851* (Cambridge, 1971). Includes information about the family's plantations in British Guiana and Jamaica.

[30] M. Craton, *Searching for the Invisible Man: Slaves and Plantation Life in Jamaica* (Cambridge, Mass., 1978). Amplifies [32].

[31] ——, 'Proto-Peasant Revolts? The Late Slave Rebellions in the British West Indies 1816–1832', *Past and Present*, LXXXV (1979).

[32] M. Craton and J. Walvin, *A Jamaican Plantation: A History of Worthy Park, 1670–1970* (1970). The first comprehensive

history of a West Indian sugar estate.

[33] S. Drescher, *Econocide: British Slavery in the Era of Abolition* (Pittsburgh, 1977). Disputes the conclusions of [37] and [40] that the plantations were in terminal economic decline before 1807. Less confident on subsequent developments.

[34] S. Engerman, 'Some Economic and Demographic Comparisons of Slavery in the United States and the British West Indies', *Economic History Review*, 2nd Series, XXIX (1976).

[35] B. W. Higman, *Slave Population and Economy in Jamaica, 1807–1834* (Cambridge, 1976). A pioneering application of statistical techniques to the subject.

[36] R. Pares, *A West-India Fortune* (1950). A Bristol merchant firm with interests on Nevis.

[37] L. J. Ragatz, *The Fall of the Planter Class in the British Caribbean, 1763–1833* (New York, 1928). The starting point for most subsequent work on the British West Indies during this period.

[38] R. B. Sheridan, '"Sweet Malefactor": The Social Costs of Slavery and Sugar in Jamica and Cuba, 1807–54', *Economic History Review*, 2nd Series, XXIX (1976). Discusses the economics of the slaves' natural reproduction.

[39] J. R. Ward, 'The Profitability of Sugar Planting in the British West Indies, 1650–1834', *Economic History Review*, 2nd Series, XXXI (1978).

[40] E. Williams, *Capitalism and Slavery* (Chapel Hill, 1944). Famous for arguing that British West Indian slavery was abolished because of its declining economic value to the mother country. Draws heavily on [37].

(iii) French West Indies

[41] C. Schnakenbourg, *Histoire de l'Industrie Sucrière en Guadeloupe aux XIXe et XXe Siècles.* Vol. I, *La Crise du Système Esclavagiste (1835–1847)* (Paris, 1980).

(iv) Cuba

[42] H. S. Klein, *Slavery in the Americas: A Comparative Study of Virginia and Cuba* (1967). Argues that the character of slavery could be influenced by cultural and legal traditions.

[43] F. W. Knight, *Slave Society in Cuba during the Nineteenth Century* (Madison, 1970). In part a critique of [42].

[44] M. Moreno Fraginals, *The Sugarmill: The Socioeconomic Complex of Sugar in Cuba 1760–1860* (New York, 1976). Emphasises the technical inflexibility of plantation slavery. For an alternative point of view see [45].

[45] R. J. Scott, 'Explaining Abolition: Contradiction, Adaptation, and Challenge in Cuban Slave Society, 1860–1886', *Comparative Studies in Society and History*, XXVI (1984).

(v) United States (For comparisons with the Caribbean. See also [34]).

[46] P. A. David *et al.*, *Reckoning with Slavery* (New York, 1976). A critique of [47].

[47] R. W. Fogel and S. L. Engerman, *Time on the Cross*, 2 vols (1974).

ADJUSTMENTS TO EMANCIPATION

(See also [2]; [6]; [11]–[25]; [79]; [85]; [95]

(i) General

[48] S. L. Engerman, 'Contract Labor, Sugar, and Technology in the Nineteenth Century', *Journal of Economic History*, XLIII (1983).

[49] W. Kloosterboer, *Involuntary Labour Since the Abolition of Slavery* (Leiden, 1960). For international comparisons.

(ii) British West Indies

[50] A. H. Adamson, *Sugar Without Slaves: The Political Economy of British Guiana, 1838–1904* (New Haven, 1972).

[51] B. Blouet, 'The Post-Emancipation Origins of the Relationships Between the Estates and the Peasantry in Trinidad', in K. Duncan and I. Rutledge (eds), *Land and Labour in Latin America* (Cambridge, 1977).

[52] O. N. Bolland, 'Systems of Domination after Slavery: The Control of Land and Labor in the British West Indies after 1838', *Comparative Studies in Society and History*, XXIII (1981). Mainly about British Honduras.

[53] B. Brereton, *Race Relations in Colonial Trinidad 1870–1900* (Cambridge, 1979).

[54] W. L. Burn, *Emancipation and Apprenticeship in the British West Indies* (1937). Concentrates on Jamaica in the 1830s.

[55] P. D. Curtin, *Two Jamaicas* (Cambridge, Mass., 1955). Emphasises social and political conflicts in the period 1815–65. See also [59].

[56] S. L. Engerman, 'Economic Adjustments to Emancipation in the United States and British West Indies,' *Journal of Interdisciplinary History*, XIII (1982).

[57] W. A. Green, 'The Planter Class and British West Indian Sugar Production, Before and After Emancipation', *Economic History Review*, 2nd Series, XXVI (1973). Argues against [37] that external factors rather than personal incapacity were the main constraints on technical innovation by sugar planters.

[58] ——, *British Slave Emancipation* (Oxford, 1976). The most comprehensive account of the British West Indies in the period 1820–65.

[59] D. Hall, *Free Jamaica 1838–1865* (New Haven, 1959). Stronger than [55] on economic developments. Takes a more optimistic view of social relations.

[60] ——, *Five of the Leewards, 1834–1870* (St. Lawrence, Barbados, 1971).

[61] ——, 'The Flight from the Estates Reconsidered: The British West Indies, 1838–42', *Journal of Caribbean History*, X–XI (1978). Argues that the ex-slaves' departure was not an instinctive reaction against the horrors of slavery.

[62] H. Johnson, 'Immigration and the Sugar Industry in Trinidad During the Last Quarter of the 19th Century', *Journal of Caribbean History*, III (1971).

[63] C. Levy, *Emancipation, Sugar and Federalism: Barbados and the West Indies, 1833–1876* (Gainesville, 1980).

[64] M. Moohr, 'Patterns of Change in an Export Economy: British Guiana, 1830–1914', unpublished Ph.D. thesis (Cambridge University, 1970).

[65] B. C. Richardson, 'Freedom and Migration in the Leeward Caribbean, 1838–48', *Journal of Historical Geography*, VI (1980).

[66] W. E. Riviere, 'Labour Shortage in the British West Indies After Emancipation', *Journal of Caribbean History*, IV (1972).

[67] W. Rodney, *A History of the Guyanese Working People, 1881–1905* (1981).

[68] D. Wood, *Trinidad in Transition* (1968). Covers the period after emancipation.

(iii) French West Indies

[69] J. Fallope-Lara, 'La Guadeloupe entre 1848 et 1900', unpublished *thèse du 3me cycle*, University of Paris IV, Sorbonne (Paris, 1972).

PROBLEMS OF ECONOMIC DEVELOPMENT

[71], [76], [87], [92] and [98] go furthest in support of dependency theory by arguing that economic underdevelopment is an inevitable result of plantations and colonial rule. [74], [89], [90], [93], [96] and [97] are most explicit in seeking to qualify this emphasis. (See also [10]–[12]; [14]; [16]–[24]; [30]; [32]; [50]; [64]; [67]; [69])

(i) General

[70] P. Bairoch and M. Lévy-Leboyer (eds), *Disparities in Economic Development since the Industrial Revolution* (1981). Includes essays by Engerman and Mandle on North America and the British West Indies.

[71] G. L. Beckford, *Persistent Poverty: Underdevelopment in Plantation Economies of the Third World* (New York, 1972). Rather casually invokes economic history in a discussion of contemporary problems.

[72] T. Birnberg and S. A. Resnick, *Colonial Development: an Econometric Study* (New Haven, 1975). Includes Cuba and Jamaica for the period c. 1890–1939.

[73] W. G. Demas, *The Economics of Development in Small Countries with Special Reference to the Caribbean* (Montreal, 1965).

[74] G. B. Hagelberg, *The Caribbean Sugar Industries: Constraints and Opportunities* (New Haven, 1974). On developments since 1945. Challenges [71].

[75] D. Lowenthal, *West Indian Societies* (1972). On the non-Hispanic Caribbean.

[76] J. R. Mandle, *Patterns of Caribbean Development* (New York, 1982). Similar in perspective to [71], but more explicitly historical.

[77] M. Proudfoot, *Britain and the United States in the Caribbean* (1954). A comparative study of recent attempts to promote economic development in Puerto Rico and the British West Indies.

[78] V. P. Timoshenko and B. C. Swerling, *The World's Sugar* (Stanford, 1957). Particularly strong on the recent history of sugar technology and international market arrangements.

(ii) British West Indies

[79] R. W. Beachey, *The British West Indies Sugar Industry in the Late Nineteenth Century* (Oxford, 1957).

[80] P. Chalmin, *Tate and Lyle, Géant du Sucre* (Paris, 1983). A history of the leading British firm of sugar refiners, the owner of plantations in the British West Indies from the 1930s. Written, unlike [92], without the benefit of much internal documentation.

[81] E. Clarke, *My Mother Who Fathered Me: A Study of the Family in Three Selected Communities in Jamaica*, 2nd edn (1966).

[82] W. L. David, *The Economic Development of Guyana 1953–1964* (Oxford, 1969).

[83] G. S. Fields, 'Employment, Income Distribution and Economic Growth in Seven Small Open Economies', *Economic Journal*, XCIV (1984). Compares the experiences of some Caribbean and East Asian territories since the 1950s to argue that the raising of wages by institutional forces may restrict economic growth and employment.

[84] O. Jefferson, *The Post-War Economic Development of Jamaica* (Kingston, Jamaica, 1972).

[85] W. K. Marshall, 'Notes on Peasant Development in the West Indies Since 1838', *Social and Economic Studies*, XVII (1968).

[86] S. B. Saul, 'The British West Indies in Depression 1880–1914', *Inter-American Economic Affairs*, XII (1958).

(iii) Cuba

[87] J. R. Benjamin, *The United States and Cuba: Hegemony and Dependent Development, 1880–1934* (Pittsburgh, 1977). Primarily about political relations, with much incidental economic information.

[88] J. I. Domínguez, *Cuba: Order and Revolution* (Cambridge, Mass., 1978). Twentieth-century history.

[89] International Bank for Reconstruction and Development (World Bank), *Report on Cuba* (Baltimore, 1951). The work of a team of economists with a well-developed historical sense.

[90] S. Lebergott, 'The Returns to U.S. Imperialism, 1890–1929', *Journal of Economic History*, XL (1980). Denies that the US exploited Cuba through investment and trade.

[91] J. O'Connor, *The Origins of Socialism in Cuba* (Ithaca, 1970). Includes economic background to the revolution of 1959. One of the most discriminating empirical studies to have been written in sympathy with dependency theory.

[92] O. Zanetti and A. Garzcía (eds), *United Fruit Company: un Caso del Domino Imperialista en Cuba* (Havana, 1976). Compare with [80]. The local archives of one of the leading US-controlled sugar concerns, expropriated after 1959, provide much interesting detail. But lack of access to the records of the firm's central administration weakens the assessment of general policy.

(iv) Puerto Rico
[93] W. Baer, 'Puerto Rico: An Evaluation of a Successful Development Program', *Quarterly Journal of Economics*, LXIX (1959). An optimistic account of Operation Bootstrap. Contrast with [98].

[94] L. W. Bergad, 'Agrarian History of Puerto Rico, 1870–1930', *Latin American Research Review*, VIII (1978). A review of the literature, modified on some points by [95].

[95] ——, *Coffee and the Growth of Agrarian Capitalism in Nineteenth-Century Puerto Rico* (Princeton, 1983).

[96] T. C. Cochran, *The Puerto Rican Businessman: a Study in Cultural Change* (Philadelphia, 1959). Includes historical material. Strongly diffusionist in its assumptions.

[97] A. D. Gayer, P. T. Homan and E. K. James, *The Sugar Economy of Puerto Rico* (New York, 1938). A detailed survey of contemporary conditions, commissioned by US sugar interests. Valuable for its attempts to confront the industry's local critics.

[98] A. López and J. Petras (eds), *Puerto Rico and Puerto Ricans: Studies in History and Society* (New York, 1974). Severely critical of US rule.

[99] L. G. Reynolds and P. Gregory, *Wages, Productivity and Industrialisation in Puerto Rico* (New York, 1965). For the 1950s.

Index